RADICAL SELF-CARE

RADICAL SELF-CARE

RITUALS FOR INNER RESILIENCE

REBECCA MOORE

Leaping Hare Press

Quarto

First published in 2024 by Leaping Hare Press,
an imprint of The Quarto Group.
One Triptych Place, London, SE1 9SH,
United Kingdom
T (0)20 7700 9000
www.Quarto.com

A catalogue record for this book is available from the British Library.

ISBN 978-0-7112-9421-9
Ebook ISBN 978-0-7112-9422-6

10 9 8 7 6 5 4 3 2 1

Design by Nicki Davis

Commissioning Editor: Monica Perdoni
Senior Editor: Laura Bulbeck
Art Director: Paileen Currie
Production Controller: Rohana Yusof

Printed in China

CONTENTS

INTRODUCTION

Welcome beautiful soul, I'm so glad you are here.

This book is a guide for radical self-care to empower and support you in creating a more conscious and sustainable life. Like many things sacred, self-care has been commodified and commercialised to the extent that many of us have lost touch with what it means. We're continuously sold the idea that we need to earn our right to rest and buy our way into wellness. Indulging in a spa break or getaway is a wonderful privilege. But if we're returning to a reality of perpetual stress and overwhelm, how effective has that time away really been? If we're not prioritising our needs regularly and consistently, how authentically are we showing up in the world? Radical self-care concerns our everyday reality and the ability to experience ourselves as powerful, capable and accountable for our health and wellness. The rituals within this book are just some of the simple but meaningful practices we can weave throughout our days to build inner resilience and help us thrive with ease.

Learning the Hard Way

Before softening into a more aligned way of living I was a raging workaholic. I had zero boundaries around my time and all the wrong ideas about what it meant to take care of myself. I took pride in my 'work hard, party harder' lifestyle. My schedule was jam-packed with exciting projects, private events and dreamy trips around the world. From the outside everything appeared to be going well for me. But below the surface, my health was crumbling. I was caught in a cycle of insistent busyness, unnerved by the thought of slowing down. After all, the more I worked, the less I had to face my increasing symptoms of stress. I would occasionally invest in a wellness treatment or class, but then spend the entire time thinking about all the work I had to get back to. Eventually, of course, I burnt out. Debilitated by mental, physical and emotional exhaustion, I was forced to take a hiatus to prioritise my healing. During this journey, I fell in love with the world of alternative medicine, discovering practices and modalities that I couldn't wait to action and share. Once I landed back on my feet, I was offered a dream job to open a wellness space in London. It felt like a brand-new lease of life, away from the relentless hustle and bustle of my previous world. However, I couldn't have been more wrong. Demands on my time and energy felt more intense than ever. I'd learned all these incredible ways of taking care of myself, but I struggled to put them into practise to support my day-to-day reality. I found myself back in burnout, depleted and bed-bound for weeks. It was a very sobering lesson: no matter the career path, industry or lifestyle we choose, stress is inevitable. We cannot get away from being challenged in life. To survive we must build inner resilience – the kind that comes only from taking exquisite care of ourselves. We must prioritise our sense of wellbeing and take steps to protect it every single day. This is the core principle of radical self-care: engaging in simple regular rituals that help us to manage stress, regulate our nervous system and keep us well. During my time writing this book, there were occasions I found myself pushing beyond my limits. There were moments when I didn't honour signs to rest or slow down. The irony, right? My inner critic is always very vocal in questioning my authority to guide others on a path that I still struggle to stay on myself. The truth is, even with the best intentions, most of us will require reminders to prioritise our wellbeing during demanding periods of our lives. We must also learn to give ourselves grace when we're not doing so well at it. Radical self-care requires the acknowledgement that perfection is a myth. We are all fallible humans, and we have to love ourselves through moments of error, repeated patterns and questionable judgement. Knowing better doesn't mean that we'll always do better. And doing the best we can is enough. So here I am, an imperfect human being, sharing these tools and ideas while still learning to put them into practice myself. Take this journey with me and let us be perfectly imperfect together.

A Moment to Pause

Before you read any further, I invite you to pause. Put the book down and take a moment to acknowledge how you are feeling. Place a hand over your heart space and a hand over your belly. Connect to the miracle of being alive in this moment. Close your eyes or lower your gaze and take three deep affectionate breaths. Gently blink open your eyes and invite your gaze back to this page. How do you feel now? Perhaps slightly calmer or more grounded than before? At our busiest, we don't always have the time or capacity to indulge in complex practices. But it's precisely at our busiest that we need to take care of ourselves the most. Small but consistent rituals can make all the difference.

The Power of Ritual

Although often associated with the traditions of a community or religion, rituals are any series of actions or types of behaviour regularly followed with a particular intention in mind. We've practised rituals since the beginning of time, to create structure in our lives, to cope with difficulty, to celebrate and acknowledge significant events and to honour rites of passage. In fact, many of the things we do daily are ritualistic in nature. Think about any conscious series of actions you follow, from the order in which you make your bed, brush your teeth and shower, to the well-timed tea or coffee breaks you schedule into your day. Or even opting for a particular route to walk home that takes you past your favourite store to pick up ingredients for dinner. Rituals are powerful because, like habits, they grow in strength over time the more they are repeated. What differentiates a ritual from a habitual routine is the awareness of what we are doing. Unlike habits, which we often do on autopilot, rituals require our attention. Radical self-care invites you to be constantly aware of what you are practising day to day, week to week, season to season, and how much these rituals support you.

Your Daily D.O.S.E.

Self-care involves carving out time to do the things that make us feel good. But let's be honest, what makes us feel good isn't always all that good for us. Particularly when we are time- and energy-poor, we are susceptible to engaging in activities that feel good in the moment, but which aren't best for us long term. Radical self-care encourages healthy ways to stimulate the chemicals in our brain that govern how we experience happiness and drive the positive emotions we feel throughout the day. Think of these four chemicals as your daily D.O.S.E. By having some understanding of how these chemicals work, we can be more deliberate in finding healthy ways to activate them:

D – Dopamine 'the pleasure chemical' is linked to motivation and reward when you complete a task, finish a project, achieve a goal or learn something new. Dopamine makes us feel good, but the effects are fleeting, which leaves us desiring more. Maintaining proper levels of dopamine is important, but because of its addictive nature, we need to be mindful about how we stimulate it.

O – Oxytocin 'the love hormone' flows when we experience meaningful eye contact or nurturing touch or spend time with people we care about. This comforting hormone can boost our immune system and make us more resistant to the addictive qualities of dopamine. Unlike dopamine, oxytocin gives us an enduring feeling of calm and safety. It can help soothe stress and promote long-lasting positive emotions.

S – Serotonin 'the mood stabiliser' can be activated by daylight, spending time in nature, embracing our emotions and practising meditation. The production of this chemical plays an essential role in many functions and processes, including sleep, digestion, bone health and more. Serotonin is also known as the 'leadership hormone' because it can be stimulated when we find opportunities to assert or prevail.

E – Endorphins 'the natural painkillers' are feel-good chemicals released through rigorous physical activity in order to diminish our perceptions of pain. Think 'runners high'. The euphoric feeling we get from endorphins is the reason movement and exercise are often prescribed to help manage stress.

Having a toolkit of radical self-care rituals that naturally boost these happiness chemicals gives us a way to get a healthy hit of our daily D.O.S.E. and avoid negative side effects. We can resource ourselves to trigger good feelings in ways that build us up rather than break us down. Over time we are less likely to lean into the vices that feel good in the moment but cause issues down the line.

Resilience Reimagined

The word 'resilience' is layered in meaning. My idea of it used to be the ability to withstand a negative or stressful situation, at all costs, even at the expense of my health. I used to think of resilience as how far I could push myself beyond my limits and the amount of times I could bounce back from burnout. I have since binned those definitions and replaced them with some that feel more aligned with my experience and more supportive of my wellbeing.

- Resilience is taking the steps to avoid burnout altogether.
- Resilience is being in touch with the truth of how we're feeling.
- Resilience is knowing and honouring our capacity and setting firm boundaries so we can give and serve from an overflowing cup.
- Resilience is the ability to remain connected to our needs during a negative or stressful situation.
- Resilience is making empowered choices of how best to support ourselves, including seeking external support when needed.
- Through radical self-care, inner resilience is created from a deep sense of inner worthiness, self-love and trust.

How to Use This Book

The following pages contain step-by-step guides to my go-to rituals for radical self-care for inner resilience, with simplicity and accessibility in mind. This collection has been inspired by the medley of modalities I discovered on my quest over the years for a happier and healthier life. I have included forty rituals, split into eight themed chapters:

Be Here Now focuses on the power of presence and includes practices that encourage us to set aside past regrets and future worries and spend more time in the NOW.

Embodiment invites us to acknowledge the wisdom we have embedded within us and offers rituals we can use to reconnect with the layers of our being.

Check In and Reflect provides tools for non-judgemental self-observation and dives into the deep inner work that helps us to move forward, grow and cultivate worthiness within.

Letting Go encourages us to recognise our unhealthy attachments and provides practices we can use to shed what is no longer serving our highest good.

Self-Soothe reminds us of the power we possess to calm and nourish ourselves through attentive actions and affirming words.

Conscious Rest delves into the types of rest we need beyond the hours of sleep we get at night and includes a few simple restorative rituals to weave into our days.

Nature's Gifts takes us back to some of the most simple and accessible support tools, relied on by our ancestors and available to us in abundance.

Togetherness encourages us to remember the significant role of community care in staying well, both for ourselves and each other. This final chapter includes rituals for connection that you can share with others.

You are welcome to work through each chapter, open a page at random or skip to the theme that will support you most in the moment. Spend time getting to know the rituals that work for you and that you truly enjoy. There is no one-size-fits-all approach for self-care, but there is something here for everyone, no matter where you are and what you have access to. Every exercise I've included can be practised within a short window of time to make it easier for you to weave into your existing daily routine. When you have the extra space for it, extend your favourite rituals to go even deeper with them. Put together a sequence to create a self-care ceremony or an at-home day retreat. The more intentional you get with creating space to take care of yourself, the more it becomes a natural way of being. I hope the ideas I am sharing with you propel you on a journey of self-discovery and a deeper experience of self-love. You are your most treasured asset, and there is nothing more important than taking care of you.

'Caring for myself is not self-indulgence,
it is self-preservation'
– Audre Lorde

I choose to be here
in this moment, *fully*
and *wholeheartedly*,
for this moment is
all there *is*.

BE HERE NOW

We spend so much time obsessing about the past or worrying about the future that we are rarely meeting life directly. Think about the moment you wake up and how quickly your mind can fill itself with thoughts about what you need to do that day. Memory and foresight are incredible gifts, but right NOW is the only place where life is *actually* happening. And if we're spending all our time living elsewhere, how much are we really living?

Being in the NOW means being fully connected to our current experience, giving it our full attention. It's a conscious awareness of the present moment. An inner spaciousness that creates an alert and coherent state. When we give the NOW our full attention, we improve the quality of what we are doing and our experience of it. It's in the NOW that we are most connected to how we feel and are best resourced to take care of ourselves.

Being rooted in the present moment puts us in touch with the truth of who we are and what we need. It allows us to follow our own rhythm and live our lives with integrity and intention. In a world of infinite distractions, presence takes practise. Begin with simple rituals like those outlined in this chapter. Over time, try to bring the same degree of awareness to any everyday activity, experiencing the sense of presence that is available at every moment as life continues to unfold.

Anchoring Breath

'Feelings come and go like clouds in a windy sky. Conscious breathing is my anchor.'

– Thich Nhat Hanh

The quickest way to connect to the present moment is to bring awareness to your breath. This is why the breath is the foundation of yoga asana and meditation practice. No matter where your focus drifts, taking just one conscious breath immediately anchors you within your body and brings you back to the here and now. Our breath is our most powerful tool for self-regulation. The way that we breathe is connected to the way that we feel, and equally, the way that we feel affects the way that we breathe. This means we have the power to transform the way that we feel by consciously altering our breath. When you are experiencing stress or feeling overwhelmed, try to observe how you are breathing and intentionally slow your breath down. Notice how this conscious awareness of your breath brings you into connection with your body and how deepening your breath invites a sense of calm. You can take an anchoring breath whenever and wherever you are, in stillness or on the move. This guided practice will deepen your awareness even further and it is a great way to come into a longer meditation.

Step 1: Find a comfortable, seated position.

Step 2: Lengthen through your spine and soften your shoulders away from your ears. Feel the connection between your seat and the earth beneath you.

Step 3: Soften your gaze, and if it feels good, gently close your eyes.

Step 4: Take a slow, deep breath in and slow, deep breath out, feeling a sense of anchoring into your body.

Step 5: Place one hand on your chest and the other over your abdomen, sensing the breath beneath your palms.

Step 6: Begin to deepen your breath even more, drawing your inhalation down into the base of your belly and extending your exhalation slightly further away.

Step 7: With each breath in, feel a gentle lightness and upward lifting energy. With every breath out allow the weight of your body to anchor towards the ground.

Step 8: Now relax your hands onto your thighs while maintaining this conscious, connected breath.

Step 9: Notice how each slow breath in creates spaciousness and each slow breath out soothes and relaxes your body.

Step 10: When the mind wanders (which it will), simply use your breath as the anchor that brings you back to your body, back to this moment and back home to yourself.

Tip: Use Dhyana mudra to enhance mindfulness and concentration when sitting with this practice. This sacred hand gesture invites the mind into a meditative state.

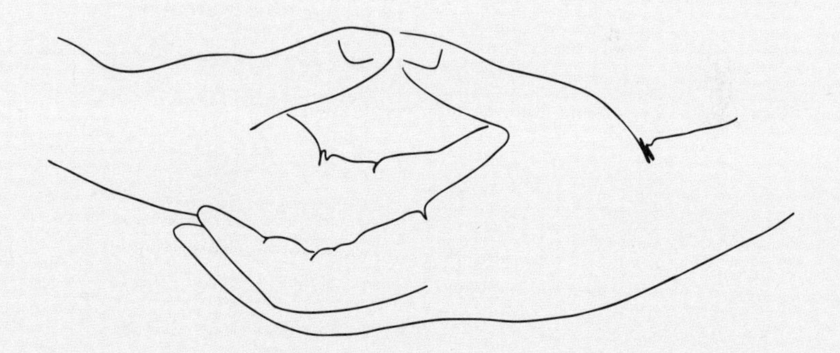

Centre of Gravity

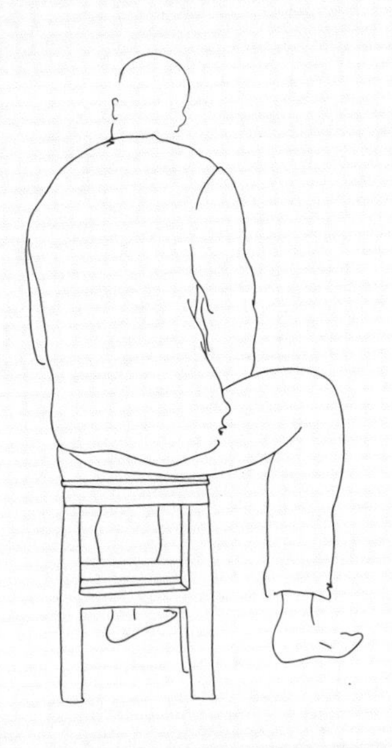

'Find your centre and stay there.'

- Barbara Ann Kipfer

Life has a habit of throwing us around. At any given moment, something beyond our control can swoop in and knock us for six. This centre of gravity ritual is inspired by an ancient technique that works to bring us back into the present moment in the midst of challenging thoughts and emotions. Popular within the practice of Aikido, the Japanese martial art of spiritual harmony, centring reconnects us to our body and helps us to feel stable and grounded within, regardless of what is happening externally.

In traditional Chinese medicine, the physical centre of gravity is the Dantian or Hara point, located just below the navel. This refers to the energy centre of physical and emotional balance and vitality. Centring works to connect us with this area so that we can feel grounded and calm. The practice only takes a couple of minutes in stillness and can be used in a moment of difficulty or before heading into a tricky situation or a sticky conversation.

Step 1: Relax your body. Find a comfortable chair and contact the ground beneath you through the soles of your feet. Roll your shoulders up and back a couple of times to release any tension. Slowly nod your head yes and then sway your head no to gently stretch and release tension from your neck and throat.

Step 2: Focus on your breathing. Close your eyes or lower your gaze, breathe in deeply through your nose and then exhale, parting your lips and making a 'shhhhhhh' sound. Repeat. Now seal your lips and come back to nasal breathing. Notice how your breath feels within your body. Breathe in for 4 counts, pause at the top for 4 counts and slowly exhale for 8 counts. Repeat for 3 rounds.

Step 3: Find your centre. Soften back into your natural flow of breathing and bring your focus to that point just a couple of inches below your navel. Place your palms there and sense grounding and stabilisation within. Once you feel this connection, release your hands and continue to feel the energy flowing in and out of your centre.

Step 4: Redirect your energy. Visualise any troubling thoughts dissolving in the flow of energy coursing through your body. As you inhale, silently say, 'I let...' and as you exhale, say, '... go.' Think about what energy you want to call on and imagine breathing it in as you repeat that word to yourself. The word could be 'strength', 'courage', 'understanding' or 'compassion' – whatever will best support you in this moment. Notice a heightened sense of balance and control.

To finish, rub your palms together and place them over your eyes. Take a deep breath in and 'shhhhhhh' your breath out. Gently open your eyes, slide your palms away and take a moment to take in your surroundings before heading back into your day.

Sense Play

'All our knowledge begins with the senses.'

- Immanuel Kant

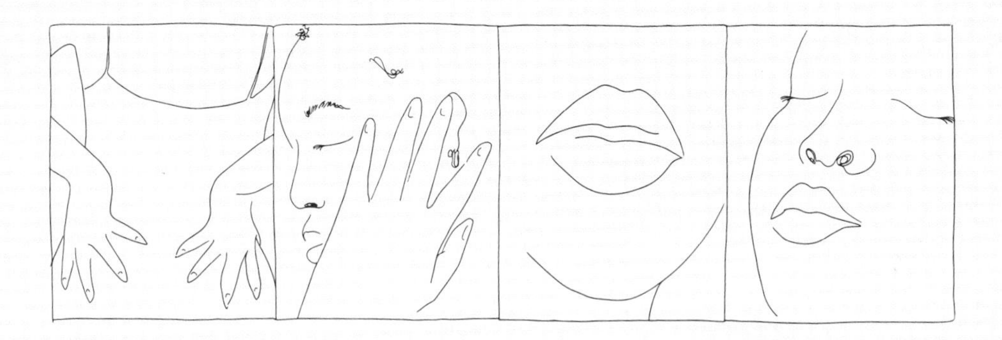

Our senses are our superpowers, helping us to understand and to perceive the world around us. Each sense gathers unique information from our environment, which is then processed by our brains to form a present-moment perception of our experience. This gives us a powerful tool for shifting our thinking and our mood in times of stress. Grounding through the engagement of our five senses is a practice commonly prescribed for relief from anxiety and is also known as the 5-4-3-2-1 method. It works by inviting you to concentrate on what is going on around you, through sight, touch, sound, smell and taste. The term 'come to your senses' literally means to regain consciousness. Intentionally engaging our senses can help calm us down and bring us back to the present moment whenever we are feeling anxious, stressed or overwhelmed. A special friend of mine also uses this practice to create core memories in her day-to-day adventures. Here's how to explore this simple grounding technique.

Step 1: Take a moment to acknowledge your thoughts and mood.

Step 2: Breathe in deeply, pause briefly, then take a slow and steady breath out.

Step 3: Begin to observe your surroundings and name out loud five things you can see. Notice any feelings or thoughts that arise in relation to what you see around you.

Step 4: Now focus on your body and name out loud four things you can feel, using your hands to touch your skin, the textures of your clothing and any objects around you. Notice any feelings or thoughts that arise in relation to what you touch.

Step 5: Become aware now of external sounds both near and far away. Name out loud three things you can hear. Notice any feelings or thoughts that arise in relation to these sounds.

Step 6: Now take a couple of curious nasal breaths and name two things that you can smell. If you can't smell anything, try to imagine two favourable smells. Notice any feelings or thoughts that arise in relation to these smells.

Step 7: Bring your focus now to your mouth and tongue. Name out loud one thing that you can taste. It might be a lingering flavour from something you've recently eaten or had to drink. Notice any feelings or thoughts that arise in relation to this taste.

Step 8: Finish with a grounding breath and acknowledge any shifts in your mood.

Tip: If your mind is racing and you're struggling to focus on your senses, try beginning with the 5–5–5 breathing technique. Inhale for 5 seconds, pause your breath for 5 seconds, and then exhale for 5 seconds. Continue for 3–6 rounds and then dive into this simple sensory exploration.

Step by Step

'The mind can go in a thousand directions,
but on this beautiful path, I walk in peace.
With each step, the wind blows.
With each step, a flower blooms.'

- Thich Nhat Hanh

Walking meditation is a mindful walking practice that brings presence both to your body and your external surroundings while engaging all of the senses. It's beneficial for people who sit for too long, as well as those who have trouble sitting still at all. As a ritual, it can be easily integrated because most of us already walk during our day. We're simply bringing mindfulness to something we do all the time without thinking about it. Walking in general is a great low-impact exercise that has incredible benefits, including energising the body and stimulating circulation. Incorporating a mindfulness practice as you walk will connect you to the present moment, allowing your mind to shift into a relaxed state improving focus, memory and clarity.

Step 1: Choose somewhere that is safe to walk and relatively peaceful.

Step 2: Before you begin to walk, take a moment to acknowledge your feelings, thoughts and mood.

Step 3: Now take an anchoring breath (see page 18) to connect to the present moment.

Step 4: Begin to walk, bringing awareness to your body and any physical sensations as you move.

Step 5: Notice your pace and slow it down slightly.

Step 6: Relax your shoulders and allow your hands and arms to swing loosely by your sides.

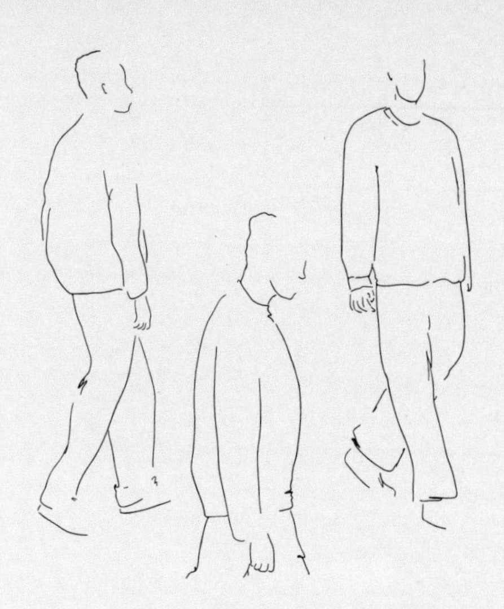

Step 7: Focus your attention on bodily sensations, such as your breath, the movement of your legs and your feet making contact with the ground.

Step 8: Observe sensations that you may normally take for granted, such as your head balanced on your neck and shoulders.

Step 9: If you notice your mind wandering, simply bring your focus back to these physical sensations.

Step 10: After about 10–15 steps, pause and take another anchoring breath.

Step 11: Now continue your walk, keeping your senses engaged and connected with your surroundings.

Step 12: Notice how it feels to breathe in the outdoor air and how the air feels on your skin. Contemplate the sounds, smells, textures and colours all around you.

Step 13: If you notice your mind wandering, simply bring your focus back to the surroundings.

Step 14: After a couple of minutes, pause again and take another anchoring breath.

Step 15: Continue to walk mindfully for as long as you wish, being aware of your body, aware of your surroundings and rooted in the here and now.

Tip: If you have mobility issues or any physical conditions that make this ritual challenging, modify or skip this practice.

Sitting with Tea

'Drink your tea slowly and reverently,
as if it is the axis on which the world
earth revolves – slowly, evenly, without
rushing toward the future.'
- Thich Nhat Hanh

Ritualised tea drinking has been around for thousands of years. Originating from China as a form of medicine, tea was introduced to Japan in the eighth century and went on to become a staple in Japanese culture before spreading far and wide. The Japanese Way of Tea or *chadō* honours the beauty in the ordinary daily routine of life, beauty we often miss. The first time I sat in a traditional tea ceremony, I was guided by the Way of Tea facilitator, LiYing Lim. Myself and other guests gazed in wonderment as LiYing performed the preparation of our tea and began serving us. During the hour-long ritual, I was exported to a realm of stillness, presence and deep appreciation that I had never quite experienced before. Tea ceremonies are a delicate art that requires training and practise, but I believe you can take the key principles and apply them to your everyday cuppa to create something profoundly beautiful for yourself. Use an intentional tea break as an opportunity to slow down, get present and appreciate your surroundings.

Step 1: Choose a tea with the qualities that best support you at the present moment; an energising tea for the morning, a soothing tea for the afternoon or a calming tea just before bed.

Step 2: Begin to prepare your tea of choice, paying close attention to the process; the sound of boiling water, the aroma that arises and the colours that are created as the tea infuses.

Step 3: Sit with your tea as you allow it to cool down, maintaining a curious awareness. Notice when your mind wanders and bring it back to the present moment.

Step 4: Once cooled to a suitable temperature, raise the cup slowly and take your first sip of tea, noticing the sensations that arise within your mouth and throughout your body.

Step 5: Allow your senses to be open without holding onto any particular thought, just a light curiosity and deep appreciation for your experience.

Step 6: Continue with this curious awareness and appreciation as you sip your tea slowly and mindfully, noticing when to pause and when to drink more.

Step 7: Once you've finished your tea, place your cup down and take a moment in gratitude for this invitation to slow down and be present.

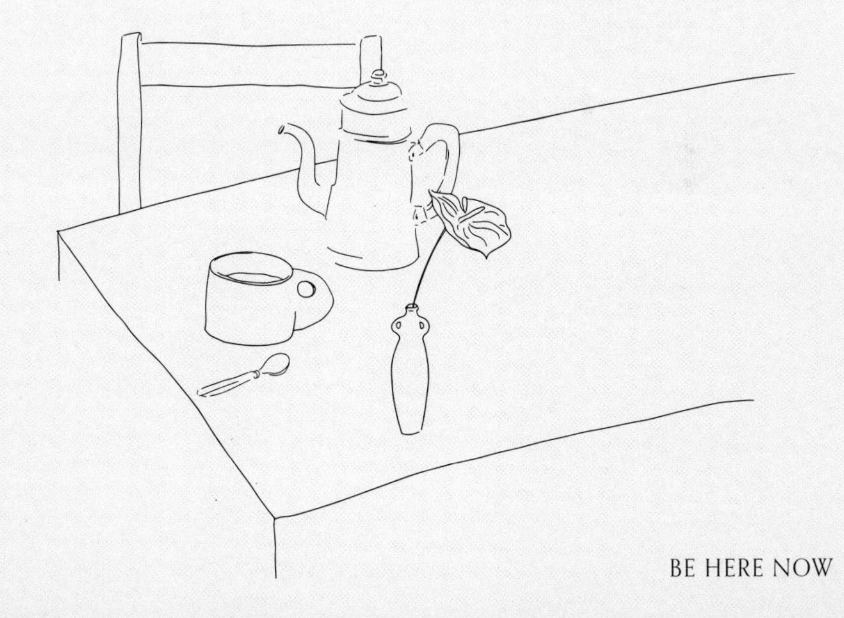

The foundation of my
being is my body.
I am *peaceful* and *whole*.
Right here, in this body,
I am *safe*.

EMBODIMENT

Our body is our home. The only place we permanently inhabit from birth until death. We have many floors and rooms in this fleshy house, and yet, many of us spend most of our time in the chaotic attics of our minds. Even when we don't feel it, what we think mentally has corresponding emotional and physical effects. Fatigue, trouble sleeping, shortness of breath and muscle tension are manifestations of stress. The more time we spend dwelling in our minds, the more we lose touch with our bodily sensations, including the messages that warn us when we are pushing ourselves too far. Embodied awareness cultivates an alert aliveness that is experienced across all the layers that make up who we are; mentally, physically, emotionally and energetically. This knowledge supports and empowers us to take better care of ourselves and helps us to better understand our boundaries and make embodied decisions based on our true capacity.

In yogic tradition, our layers of being are described as the five koshas. The first is the physical body that houses all the other layers, which we experience by touching and sensing it. The second, the energy body, keeps us alive and is experienced through our breathing and circulation. The third is the mental and emotional layer, which we experience through our thoughts, feelings and input from our five senses. The fourth layer represents our higher intelligence and the fifth is our spiritual body, which can be experienced as deep contentment or bliss. The embodiment practices in this chapter aim to bring us back to the sensitivity we need to experience the multiple layers of our being. To reconnect with each layer, or room, in our internal home and get to know ourselves better, from the inside out.

In My Body

'The body always leads us home ... if we can simply learn to trust sensation and stay with it long enough for it to reveal appropriate action, movement, insight, or feeling.'
- Pat Ogden

Taking care of our bodies means spending more time in them. Experiencing ourselves fully, from the crown of our heads to the tips of our toes. Aligning our mind, body and breath creates present-moment awareness, reconnecting us to our feelings and releasing physical and emotional tension. This body-scan meditation takes you into an in-depth analysis, inviting you to pay close attention to emotional and physical sensations that arise and connect deeper to the more subtle layers of your being. You can practise this either seated or lying down.

Step 1: Relax in a comfortable position of your choice and notice the surface beneath you.

Step 2: Begin to shift your awareness from the outside world to your internal landscape.

Step 3: Take a moment to fully arrive in your body and connect to your breath. Notice how your breath feels within your body as it fills you up and then leaves your lungs empty.

Step 4: Now bring your attention down to your feet, observing any sensations. You may want to wiggle your toes or slowly move your ankles to deepen your awareness of your feet.

Step 5: Move your attention up your legs, observing any sensations within your calves, knees and thighs. Imagine breathing into and out of your legs and invite any tension to soften and release.

Step 6: Now move your focus to your lower back and pelvis, softening your glutes and observing the connection between your body and the surface beneath you.

Step 7: Shift your focus to your stomach, sensing your internal organs and observing the breath as it fills and empties your lungs.

Step 8: Bring your attention to your chest area, perhaps tuning into your heartbeat. Observe your chest rising and falling as you breathe.

Step 9: On your next breath out, shift your awareness to your hands, observing any sensations here. You might want to wiggle your fingers or slowly move your wrists to deepen your awareness of your hands.

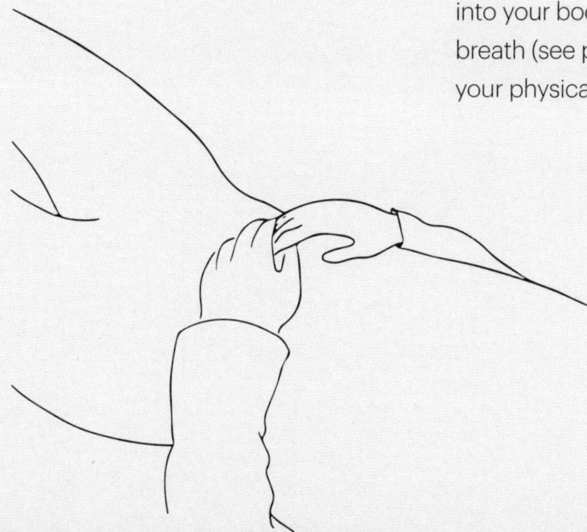

Step 10: Allow this awareness to travel up your arms and into your shoulders and neck, observing any sensations and using your breath to soften and relax your body.

Step 11: Now direct your attention to your head, scalp and face. Notice how your head feels on top of your shoulders and the way your breath enters and exits through your nose.

Step 12: Let your awareness expand across your entire body, from the top of your head down to the tips of your toes. Feel the natural rhythm of your breath. Feel your entire body alive and present.

Step 13: To finish, gently begin to stretch into your body, take a deep anchoring breath (see page 18) and come back to your physical surroundings.

Seated Spirals

'We see in order to move; we move in order to see.'
- William Gibson

If you're feeling foggy in the mind or heavy in the body, stir things up with Sufi grinds. Often used as a warm-up practice in Kundalini yoga, this technique involves an active rotation of the torso in both clockwise and anticlockwise directions, in coordination with the breath. The consciously connected movement cultivates a soft embodied awareness with energy-boosting benefits. It's a slow and sensual practice that works like a massage for your internal organs, stirring up and spreading happy hormones throughout your body. You can practise Sufi grinds as a pre-meditation ritual, as part of a longer movement routine or as a stand-alone practice for connection and joy.

Step 1: Begin in a comfortable, seated position and take a few anchoring breaths (see page 18) to drop into your body and be present.

Step 2: Place your hands on your knees, lengthen through your spine and relax your shoulders.

Step 3: Holding your knees for support, begin to make big circles with your upper body moving in a clockwise or counterclockwise direction.

Step 4: Coordinate your movement with your breath, inhaling to come forwards and exhaling as you circle back.

Step 5: When you feel ready, shut your eyes and drop into the sensation of the movement.

Step 6: Keep rotating your torso for about 60 seconds and then switch directions.

Step 7: Pay close attention to how your body feels in this movement.

Step 8: Notice any difference in sensations in this direction.

Step 9: Keep the circles connected to your breath, inhaling as you move forwards and exhaling as you circle back.

Step 10: After another 60 seconds have passed, slowly come back to an upright position.

Step 11: Finish with an inhale for 4 counts, a pause for 4 counts and a slow exhale for 8 counts.

Step 12: Keep your eyes closed for another 60 seconds if you can, sitting still and feeling the rush of happy hormones flowing through your body.

Caution: Avoid this practice if you've had abdomenal surgery or experienced any conditions that affect the internal organs or spine.

Wake-up Call

*'The biggest reason for our existence
is to feel the rapture of being alive.'*
- Lebo Grand

In traditional Chinese medicine, meridians are the energetic pathways within the body where the qi, or chi, flows. Similar to prana as described in yogic tradition, qi or chi are the Chinese Daoists terms for the 'vital life force' or 'life energy', present in all human beings and all life in the universe. Rather than the Chakra system in yogic tradition, traditional Chinese medicine considers our internal organs as the main focus points of energy storage and distribution. There are believed to be 12 principal meridians, each associated with an organ; the heart, pericardium, lung, spleen, liver and kidney (the yin organs), and the stomach, gallbladder, large and small intestine, urinary bladder and tri-heater or triple burner (the yang organs). Yin organs function to store energies, while Yang organs function to transform and transmit energies. If the flow of this life force energy becomes blocked or imbalanced in any way, it can have serious consequences on health. Each meridian is also linked to a particular element and different emotions. Emotional imbalance is often a sign of unbalanced qi (or chi). Like acupuncture, meridian body slapping works to stimulate cells, improve circulation and balance the flow of life force energy to support our wellbeing.

I spent a transformative week exploring Meridian Yoga Therapy with Science of Self founder Dr Rose Erin Vaughan. Each movement practice begins with a meridian body-slapping technique to awaken the muscles and activate energy. I nicknamed this ritual the Wake-Up Call because of the feeling of embodied aliveness it creates. You use the palms of the hands to slap the large surfaces of the body below the shoulders and the fingertips to tap the neck, head and face. Lose fists are used for the pelvis, sacrum and glutes.

The practice starts with a front-of-body activation along the stomach meridian pathway.

Step 1: Begin slapping the top of the feet and front of the ankle, moving up the shins and across the front of the thighs.
Step 2: Make loose fists with your hands and gently pound the front of the hips, moving up to the abdomen with slightly more force.
Step 3: Now release your fists and slap across the front ribs and chest.
Step 4: Use your fingertips to tap behind the collarbones and up the throat.
Step 5: Tap the corners of your mouth and just beneath the eyes.
Step 6: Repeat the journey all the way back down to the feet.

Now move to the sides of the body for activation along the gallbladder meridian pathway.

Step 1: Begin slapping the sides of the ankles, moving up the sides of the legs and thighs.
Step 2: Make loose fists with your hands and gently pound the sides of the hips.
Step 3: Now release your fists and slap the sides of the waist and the ribcage.
Step 4: Slap the tops of the shoulders and, using your fingertips, tap up the sides of the neck.
Step 5: Tap along the sides of the jaw and just above the ears.
Step 6: Repeat the journey all the way back down to the feet.

Finish with a back body activation along the bladder meridian pathway.

Step 1: Begin slapping the heels, moving up to the calves and across the backs of the thighs.
Step 2: Make loose fists to pound the glutes and sacrum.
Step 3: Continue up the lower back (avoiding the spine).
Step 4: Now release your fists and slap across each shoulder onto the upper back.
Step 5: Use your fingertips to tap up the back of the neck and the base of the skull.
Step 6: Tap on the crown of the head and then the forehead and eyebrows.
Step 7: Repeat the journey all the way back down to the feet.

To end, stand still for a few seconds with the eyes closed and sense the energy moving underneath your skin.

The Archer

'The world needs warriors of love.
Take up your arms with insight,
presence and compassion.
Go out there to fight the good fight
gently, bravely, decently.'
- Unknown

If you've ever practised a Warrior pose in a yoga class, you may have experienced the powerful essence it evokes. A primordial feeling of courage and strength washes over you as you stand firm with the entire body engaged. Standing Archer pose shares these bold and empowering qualities. Often practised in Kundalini yoga, it promotes a good flow of energy through what is called our 'radiant body', while building physical and mental strength. Our radiant body is the sublime inner light that projects our radiant essence out into the world around us. The Archer pose strengthens the qualities of this radiance; courage, creativity and nobility, regardless of obstacles and fear.

You don't need a yoga mat to practise the Archer. Just remember to remove your socks if you are in a space with a slippery floor.

Step 1: Create a strong foundation. Take a moment to stand still with the feet together, feeling a connection with the ground beneath you. Step your right foot forwards, about 1 metre (3 feet) in front of your left, keeping both feet parallel and toes pointing straight ahead. Turn your left heel in and swivel your left toes outwards to the left side, keeping your heel on the ground. With your left leg straight behind you, bend your right knee into a lunge. Do not let the knee overshoot your toes. Adjust your position if necessary. Ensure your spine is straight and your tailbone is pointing towards the floor. Engage your core and feel a sense of stability and groundedness through both legs.

Step 2: Draw your bow. Bring both arms straight out in front of you, palms facing. Curl the fingers of both hands into the palms, thumbs pulled back. As if pulling back a bow and arrow, draw the left arm back, bending into the left elbow until your left fist meets your left shoulder. You should feel an opening stretch across your chest. Keep both shoulders relaxed and arms engaged.

Step 3: Fix your gaze. Bring your chin down slightly, keep your eyes open and gaze beyond your right thumb as if you were looking out into infinity. Hold here for 1–3 minutes, taking deep long breaths.

Step 4: To switch sides, straighten your right leg, relax your arms down and step your feet back together. Give yourself a moment to feel your body, and the breath and life inside of you. Now step your left foot forwards and repeat the posture on the opposite side.

Step 5: When you're done, gently come out of the posture, step your feet back together and stand tall and still for another minute or so, feeling the sensations within your body and the expansion of energy radiating from you.

Tip: To quieten down a busy mind and enjoy an extra boost of energy, replace long, deep breaths with The Breath of Fire (see page 72).

Groundwork

'Your body is the ground metaphor of your life, the expression of your existence.'
- Gabrielle Roth

No exercise feels better than moving your body in the way that your body wants to move and being intuitively guided into a stretch or a twist, a roll or a fold. Moving curiously with an openness and a deep inward awareness is the magic of somatic therapy.

The term 'somatic' means 'embodied' or 'of the body'. Somatic practice involves body-led movements that focus on your internal experience. The movement doesn't need to make sense or look graceful in any way. What matters is whole-body connectivity and how each movement feels from the inside out.

Moving with the floor creates safety and support for embodied exploration. It's restorative, calming and relaxing. Regular practise can shift patterns of chronic stress and improve mobility and strength, while creating greater body awareness.

You don't need a yoga mat for this practice. Direct connection with the floor is encouraged, but feel free to use blankets and cushions for comfort if necessary.

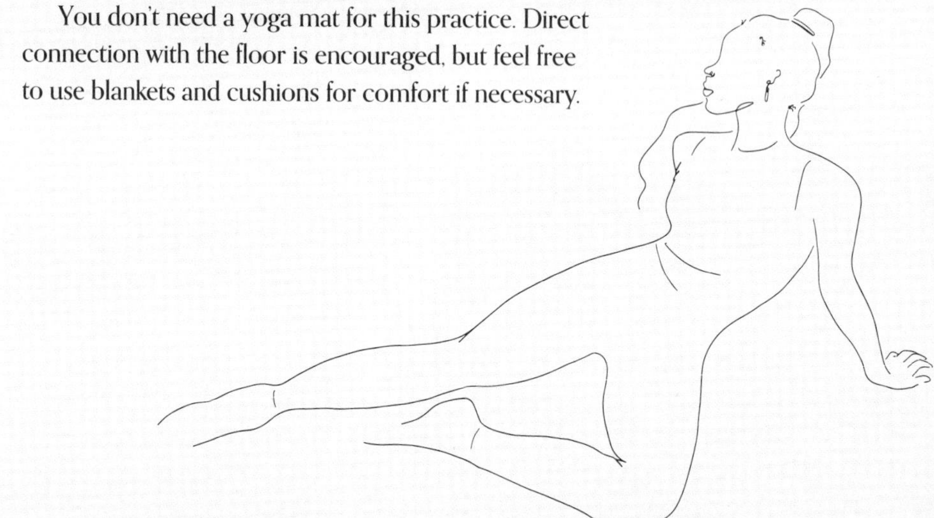

Step 1: Lie flat on your back with your knees bent and the soles of your feet in contact with the ground, arms resting beside your body.

Step 2: Gently adjust your position until you feel comfortable enough to be still. Keep your eyes open or closed, as you wish.

Step 3: Take 1–2 minutes to fully arrive in your body and connect to your breathing, observing how your breath feels within your body and how your body moves as you breathe.

Step 4: Now observe how it feels to lie flat on the ground. Scan your entire body, noticing where you are tense and where you are at ease. Move gently into any areas of tightness and notice if that creates some space.

Step 5: Begin to gently arch your back, bringing your belly upward and pressing your glute muscles and feet into the floor. Then, slowly lower your back and flatten it against the floor. Repeat this movement very slowly, scanning the muscles in your torso for any tension and inviting release.

Step 6: Now stretch your legs out in front of you and raise your arms overhead. Point your toes away from you and then towards you, feeling a stretch in your ankles and legs.

Step 7: Lengthen your right leg and left arm as if someone is pulling you in opposite directions. Relax back to neutral and then repeat on the other side, stretching your left leg and right arm. Return to neutral once again.

Step 8: Explore any other areas of your body with intuitive movement. Be slow and gentle, maintaining curiosity and embodied awareness.

Step 9: Finish with an affirming mantra: 'I'm safe inside this container called me.'

I *accept* and *embrace*
all of my humanness.
My sensitivity is a *gift*
and all of my feelings
are valid.

CHECK IN AND REFLECT

It's so easy to get caught up in the hustle and bustle of everyday life, focusing on the next place we need to be or the next thing we need to do. Despite all that our lives demand of us, to take radical care of ourselves, we have to carve out the time to check in and reflect. Without careful self-assessment, we may bypass what we truly feel and need. We're also more likely to get caught in destructive emotional patterns and stress can become our regular state.

Checking in connects us to the truth of how we're feeling in the moment, helping us to identify our fluctuating emotions and needs, and how best to meet them. We can then be more intentional with our actions and make decisions that work for us rather than against us. Reflection invites us to look back and gain a better understanding of who we are and what's most important to us. With non-judgemental observation, we can analyse past situations and behaviours and learn from them. We can celebrate our achievements and be honest about what hasn't worked out so well for us and why. We can gain clarity on what is driving us forward and anything that may be holding us back.

Check-in and reflection rituals keep us in a constant state of learning and expanding, strengthening our emotional intelligence and wisdom of what it means to be human. The key is to practise self-observation without judgement. Whatever we notice about ourselves should be met with openness and compassion. So much of our lives are spent trying to be better or different in some way; it's important to create spaces for ourselves where we can be exactly as we are. Sitting with our feelings and looking back at past experiences can be uncomfortable and confronting. This chapter aims to give you some guiding support.

Layers of Being

'When we are grounded in our awareness, we can be more present with what we are experiencing in our bodies – in all the spaces that live between our head and our feet.'
– Raegan Robinson

Our body is an ecosystem, made up of various layers, both material and energetic, all working in agreement with each other. In yogic philosophy, these layers of being are described as the five koshas. Annamaya kosha is the physical layer made up of all the physical structures in our body. Pranamaya kosha is the layer of our life force energy, perceived through breath and circulation. Manomaya kosha is the psychological layer through which we experience feelings and thoughts. Vijnanamaya kosha is the layer of our higher intelligence and Anandamaya kosha is our spiritual core. It is believed that to live a healthy and balanced life, all these layers need to be kept in good condition. This meditation practice invites you to acknowledge each of these layers that make you whole.

Step 1: Find a comfortable position either seated or lying down.

Step 2: Draw your awareness inward and begin to cultivate a curiosity about your experience. Notice what you sense here, releasing any judgements of good or bad, right or wrong.

Step 3: Bring your curious awareness to the first layer of your being, the Annamaya kosha, acknowledging how it feels to be within your physical body in this moment. Notice any areas of tension, paying particular attention to your face and jaw, and the base of the neck and shoulders. Notice where your body meets the ground and how comfortable you are in this moment. Make any adjustments you need.

Step 4: Now bring your curious awareness to your energy body, the Pranamaya kosha, by connecting with your breath. Follow the journey of your breathing as it flows in and out of your body, noticing any areas where the breath feels restricted. Notice where each inhalation ends and your exhalation begins.

Step 5: Shift your awareness now to your psychological layer, the Manomaya kosha, acknowledging how you are feeling emotionally and observing any inner thoughts, quiet or loud. Without attaching to any one thought or feeling, be curious about any patterns or themes that arise. Notice what is guiding your feelings and thoughts in this moment.

Step 6: Now see if you can sense your higher intelligence, the Vijnanamaya kosha, that deep knowing within yourself. The layer of inner wisdom beneath your fears and doubts. Breathe deeply into this space, whether you sense it or not. With every breath, anchor deeper into trust.

Step 7: Finally, see if you can drop your awareness even deeper, into the core of who you are, the Anandamaya kosha. Surrender into the spaciousness beyond the body and the mind. Breathe deeply here and feel a sense of interconnection with all that exists.

Step 8: Sit with yourself for as long as you wish. When you are ready to close the practice, breathe your awareness back through all five layers of your being until you are grounded back into your physical body.

Tip: Once you get the hang of this practice, explore it in movement. Try it when you are walking or dancing. Notice how different activities and environments create deeper connections to specific layers.

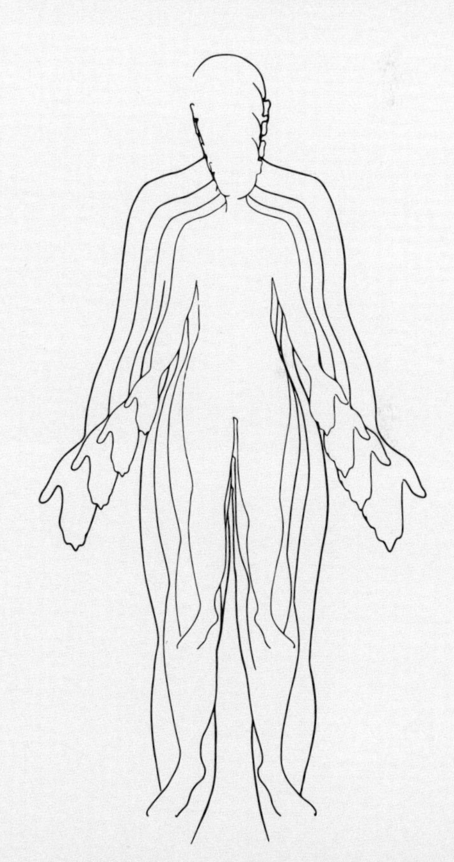

Feeling Feelings

'Our feelings are not there to be cast out or conquered. They're there to be engaged and expressed with imagination and intelligence.'

- T.K. Coleman

We are divine beings, here on earth to experience what it's like to be human; the joy, the excitement, the sadness, the grief. We are here to feel it all. Unfortunately for many of us, instead of learning how to be with our feelings, we are taught how to mask and repress them. This is the main cause of tension and imbalance in the body. To stay well, we need to feel our feelings. Embracing more difficult emotions can be hard, but everything we feel is communicating something to us for our highest good. Fear may be a call to find safety. Anger may be a call for action or a reminder to create firmer boundaries. Sadness may be a calling to heal and be held. We must learn how to sit with our feelings and listen with love.

This ritual is inspired by the work of Dr Paul Ekman, who I discovered through the Museum of Happiness. It can be practised both as a self-check-in and self-reflective technique. You'll need a pen and a journal or paper to make notes.

Take a moment to tune into how you are feeling in this present moment, or a feeling you have recently experienced. Use the prompts below to journal about the messages your emotions could be trying to communicate. Have a conversation with your feelings, as if they are your allies, helping to guide you in the right direction.

Hello sadness – How can I best take care of you?
Hello anger – What change needs to take place? What boundary needs to be set?
Hello guilt – What do I need to let go of?
Hello disgust – What do I need to move away from?
Hello joy – How can we create more space for you?

Explore these prompts with curiosity and compassion, avoiding the urge to judge feelings as good or bad, right or wrong. Practice with mindfulness, noticing the thoughts that are present and the feelings those thoughts create. Be aware also of any corresponding sensations in the body. Listen with love and make note of any messages that come up from deep within yourself. Know that just being attentive in this way is medicine in itself. When you've finished journaling, read this reminder out loud:

I am here to feel
And life is here to be lived
In all its intensity.
The pain that leaves me breathless
And the beauty that takes my breath away,
I must leave room for it all.

Tip: If challenges arise for you during this practice, do whatever you need to best take care of yourself, whether that's reaching out for support, further reflection or rest.

Daily Desires

'Knowing how you actually want to feel is the most potent form of clarity that you can have.'
- Danielle LaPorte

We often set our sights on external goals and achievements. But what if we spent more time focused on the internal feelings that we'd like to experience and be guided forward from that place? I was first introduced to the concept of desire mapping back in 2017. So much of my life up to that point had been guided by material accomplishments and external expectations. Created by Danielle LaPorte, the Desire Map method seeks to prioritise how we want to feel over what we want to achieve. Through it, I learned to make decisions and plans based on the feelings I most desired to experience. Rather than ruminating on future-focused goals and constantly questioning my purpose in life, I started to live each day with more intention and allow my purpose to unfold through the expression of who I am.

Inspired by the Desire Map method, here's an intention-setting ritual you can practise in the morning to bring more awareness to your feelings and to create external experiences that support those desired feelings.

Step 1: Take a moment to acknowledge your mood and any thoughts or feelings you've woken up with.

Step 2: Now take a few anchoring breaths (see page 18) to drop into your body. Allow your thoughts and feelings to become weightless and focus your attention on the spaciousness within.

Step 3: Ask yourself the gentle enquiry: 'How do I want to feel today?'

Step 4: Now, using a pen and paper or journal, write down what comes to mind. Include as many desired feelings as you can without thinking too much.

Step 5: Look at your list and choose three core feelings that you'd like to experience the most.

Step 6: Set two intentions for your day that reflect these core feelings.

Step 7: Now decide on just one action you can take to awaken your core feelings and embody your intentions. Here are a few example of entries:

Peaceful, Content and Connected.
My intentions are to slow down and be present.
I will find a park or garden and take 10 minutes to be with nature.

Joyful, Creative and Expansive.
My intentions are to practise gratitude and to look for the beauty in everything I experience.
I will put on music and dance like no one is watching.

Nourished, Loved and Supported.
My intentions are to speak kindly to myself and listen to my body.
I will prepare myself a simple, wholesome meal.

Tip: Over time, notice the desired feelings that keep recurring for you. Create a go-to list of simple things that generate these desired core feelings, which serve as easy ways to connect with the way you want to feel.

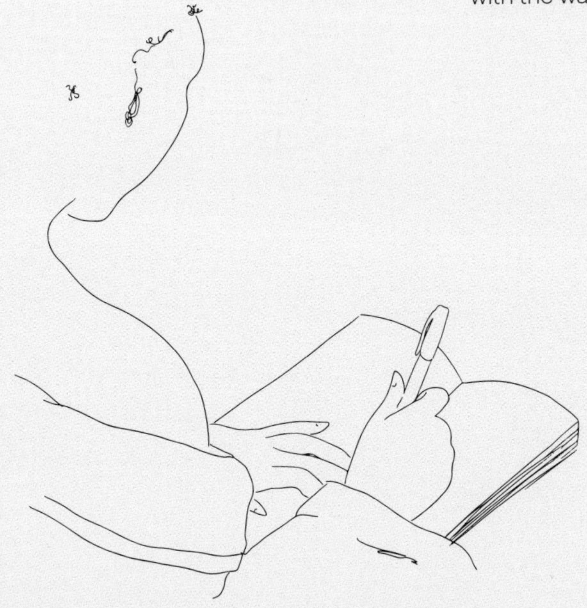

Life Inventory

'I want my life to be a reflection of the love I have for myself.'
- Shannon Rae Lawes

Moving forwards in the right direction requires looking back. When we carefully observe our past and present experiences, we can see more clearly what is and isn't aligning with who we are. Priorities become clearer. A light is shone on where we are overextending and areas that require more of our energy and attention. This life inventory ritual is a self-reflection practice that aims to bring you back to yourself and what matters to you the most. It invites you to take stock of what has been, what could be, what needs to be tended to or resolved and what you can do right now to put your best foot forward.

Step 1: Begin by creating a comfortable nest for yourself. Sit at a desk, on the sofa, or on the floor. If needed, wrap a blanket around you to keep you warm. If possible, place a couple of meaningful objects close by.

Step 2: Take a moment to tune into your internal landscape. Close your eyes or lower your gaze and observe the thoughts and feelings that are alive for you right now. Silence the outside noise and allow your awareness to sink even deeper within.

Step 3: Begin to reflect on the dreams and goals you have for yourself. Tune into your heart's desires and how they are currently being met. Curiously and compassionately observe the thoughts and feelings these reflections evoke.

Step 4: When you're ready, gently blink your eyes open and return to your space. Using a pen and paper or your journal to write on, explore the following prompts:

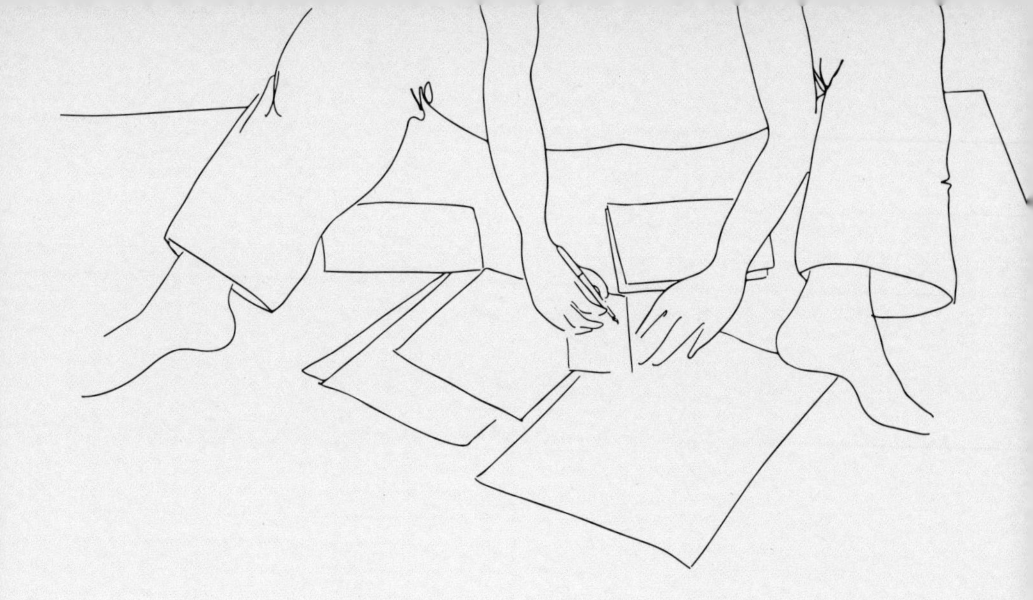

Looking back, what has been working in my favour? What has not and why?
Where can I create more balance in my life?
What unresolved issues do I need to carve out some time to handle?
What has been on the back burner for too long?
Where can I expand into new waters?
What dreams are alive for me right now?
What in my life can I revisit with new eyes?
What simple shift might have a powerful impact if I go ahead and make it today?

Step 5: Finish this practice by taking a few anchoring breaths (see page 18) to drop into your body and connect to the present moment.

Tip: Explore this practice with openness and compassion. Finish by listing three things that you celebrate about yourself and three people you are most grateful for.

Shadow Work

'There is no greater journey than the one that you must take to discover all of the mysteries that lie within you.'
- Michelle Sandlin

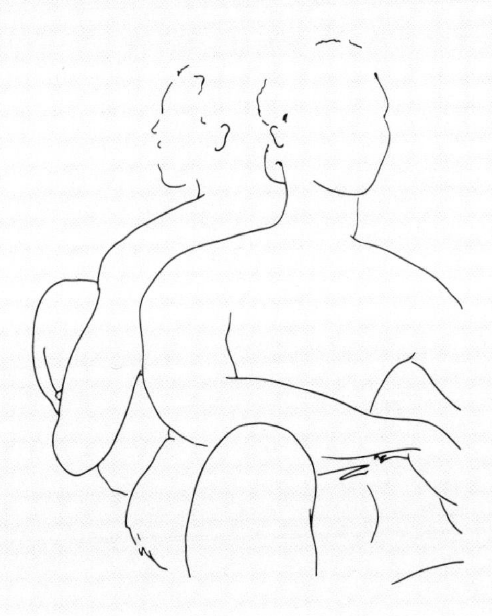

As beneficial as it is to regard ourselves highly, it is also important to acknowledge the aspects we deem less favourable. The person we choose to show to the world has what author Thomas Moore calls a 'dark double', composed of the parts of ourselves that we subconsciously reject. This is referred to in Jungian psychology as our shadow self. As psychoanalyst Carl Jung explains in his book *Aion* (1951), 'To become conscious of it involves recognising the dark aspects of the personality as present and real. This act is the essential condition for any kind of self-knowledge.'

Shadow work isn't easy of course. It forces us to confront the repressed parts of ourselves that we try so hard to hide. But it also enables us to get to the root cause of our triggers, emotional reactions and even symptoms of stress and anxiety. Our inner shadow is part of who we are and craves to be explored and understood. Shadow work develops our self-awareness and helps us to integrate all parts of who we are with acceptance and compassion. When we better understand how the more hidden aspects of ourselves influence our behaviour, we are more empowered to live life consciously and authentically.

Freewriting is a great way to express the different sides of who you are. You can practice this by scribbling down whatever comes up without overthinking it. You can also use the following reflective prompts for exploration.

When I think about the future, what am I the most afraid of? What is the worst that could happen?

How do I believe people see me? How would they describe me to someone else? How does that make me feel?

What makes me most self-conscious?

What traits do I see in people that I wish I had myself?

When am I most judgemental towards others and why?

Where am I being too hard on myself? Where does it stem from?

When was the last time I was triggered? What can I learn about myself from that experience? Which lesson am I most reluctant to learn?

What are the stories I tell myself that cause me pain? What can I do to rewrite them?

What memories am I most ashamed of? How can I let them go?

When was the last time I forgave myself?

What are the patterns I'm repeating that are keeping me stuck?

What habits am I currently devoted to and how do they serve me?

What are my conflicting desires and how can I create more harmony between them?

Tip: Remember that shadow work is designed to be confronting. It takes courage. Explore with curiosity, openness and compassion. If you struggle to answer the prompts with words, try drawing your feelings instead.

I *release* anything creating constriction in my journey. I forgive and let go. I *surrender* and *flow*.

LETTING GO

Life requires us to let go, over and over again. And yet, it's probably one of the hardest things to do. By nature, we are clingy creatures, holding onto things even when they weigh us down, from draining relationships, stressful jobs and unresolved emotions to unhealthy thought patterns and behaviours. Our attachments create both an illusion of control and a fear of the unknown, so it can often feel safer to cling to what feels familiar. But if we want to grow and evolve, we need to become intentional about releasing what keeps us from moving forwards.

Our decisions shape our lives and what we choose to hold onto impacts our experience. Remaining in any situation or state that is causing us stress will take its toll on our wellbeing. The emotional baggage we carry around as a result impedes our presence, our peace of mind and our ability to show up in the world fully and authentically. We must wilfully release what doesn't belong to us anymore.

Much of what we're taught is good for us is easier said than done. Letting go is no exception. Saying goodbye requires us to grieve what we're leaving behind, which can be an emotionally charged and uncomfortable process. It's very hard to let go of things we care about or that provide us with comfort. But we need to trust our inner compass and let go of anything creating constriction in our journey. Over time, the practice of letting go makes us more adaptable and resilient, increasing our ability to cope with uncertainty and change. When nothing is known for sure, everything is possible. With nothing to hold onto, there is nothing to lose. Life requires us to let go, over and over again.

Sacred Tears

'I no longer fear the stream of unexpected tears, for I know now it's my heart's way of cleansing itself.'

- Rebecca Moore

We are all sensitive beings, filled to the brim with emotions, whether we choose to express them or not. When we've been shamed for our tears, we learn to put limits on them or hold them all inside. But crying is healing and healthy. Our sacred tears enable us to release emotional tension that can build up. These tears are an expression of the relief that comes when we've allowed ourselves to really feel something, whether that be grief, frustration, gratitude or joy. Our tears ensure that our most vulnerable emotions can be felt.

In folk tradition, crying was regarded as more than a spontaneous expression of feeling; it was also a language and means of communication. In the words of the writer and essayist Washington Irving, 'There is a sacredness in tears. They are not the mark of weakness but of power. They speak more eloquently than ten thousand tongues. They are the messengers of overwhelming grief, of deep contrition, and of unspeakable love.'

Although it's not always easy, we must encourage our emotions to move through us, so they don't get stuck. Suppressing our tears increases stress levels in the body and contributes to physical symptoms like pain and fatigue. When we hold in emotional tension for too long, it can manifest into unresolved trauma. It's important to create containers that allow you to feel the full extent of your feelings and invite them to flow out. Here are some ways to find those spaces.

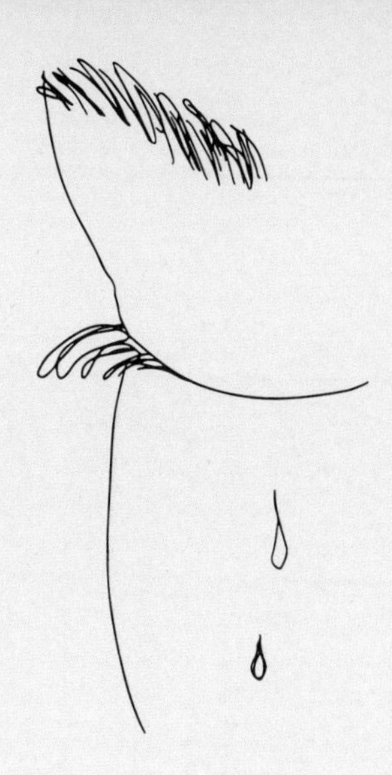

In private

Find a quiet space that is free from distractions and the opinions of others to allow you the privacy and safety to feel your emotions deeply enough to release them.

In water

Water is cleansing and nurturing, which can help to encourage feelings to be felt and expressed. Inviting sacred tears to flow in the shower or bath can leave you feeling both physically and emotionally refreshed.

To music

The limbic system, which is involved in processing emotions and controlling memory, lights up when our ears perceive music. That's why we feel music so deeply. Playing a slow melancholic song can help release the valve for tears to flow.

In nature

Nature doesn't judge us but instead invites us to be who we are. Going for a walk or sitting under a tree can offer a safe space to cry. Being in nature also helps restore the internal balance that gets thrown off when we're going through an intense emotional release.

With a friend

It's easy to feel the least understood when experiencing our heaviest emotions. This can be the hardest time to reach out for support. Sharing your words and your tears with someone you trust can relieve the weight you are feeling.

Vulnerability requires safety. Wherever you find space for your sacred tears to flow, clear your mind of distractions and allow yourself to be with the emotion you're experiencing. Let it rise up and flow out. When your tears arrive, don't resist them. Notice how you feel when they dry up. It may not always be joy and happiness, but you're likely to feel a bit lighter and freer than before.

Shaking It Out

'There is more wisdom in your body than in your deepest philosophy.'
– Friedrich Nietzsche

Stressful situations can trigger our fight, flight or freeze response, a set of survival instincts developed by our ancient ancestors many years ago to stay alive. When this happens, our bodies physiologically prepare us for matters of life or death. The trouble occurs when the situation doesn't require us to fight, run away or even freeze and we're left with a tank full of adrenaline and cortisol that has nowhere to go. Shaking therapy is a way to release and reset the survival energy that gets trapped in our bodies. It activates the parasympathetic nervous system, sending signals to the brain to calm down, relax and let go. Shaking can be practised following a stressful event or to release lingering negative energy from another person or place.

Step 1: Stand with your feet hip-width apart and relax your knees.

Step 2: Take a moment to acknowledge how you are feeling.

Step 3: Feel your feet firmly rooted on the ground, and sense that you are supported.

Step 4: Now take a deep breath in and as you exhale, relax your shoulders and allow your arms to hang heavy.

Step 5: Begin to bounce through your knees and gradually allow the vibration to spread up your body into your arms and shoulders.

Step 6: Allow the shaking to spread into any parts of your body that want to participate. Begin slowly so you can stay connected to your body and feel any pent-up energy being discharged.

Step 7: Pause and check in: how do you feel? What has shifted?

Tip: You can set a timer, play a song or simply shake until your body feels ready to stop.

Forgiveness Mantra

'The practice of peace and reconciliation is one of the most vital and artistic of human actions.'

– Thich Nhat Hanh

Inner resentments, big or small, towards ourselves or others are burdensome feelings to carry. They keep us focused on the past, which clouds our vision for the future. They create tension within the body and make it hard for us to relax. To gain freedom from hurt, anger, disappointment or guilt, we have to let forgiveness in.

Ho'oponopono is a powerful healing mantra that originates from Hawaii. Traditionally practised by indigenous Hawaiian healers, this ancient ritual is used for both forgiveness towards others and forgiveness towards oneself. The word *ho'oponopono* roughly translates as 'to cause things to move back in balance' or 'to make things right.' Chanting the ho'oponopono mantra repeatedly is a powerful way to release shame, guilt, ill will or any other feelings that keep our minds fixated on negative thoughts. There are four components to the mantra:

The first is to accept responsibility – '*I'm sorry*.'
The second is to ask for forgiveness – '*Please forgive me*.'
The third is to give thanks – '*Thank you*.'
The fourth is to express your love – '*I love you*.'

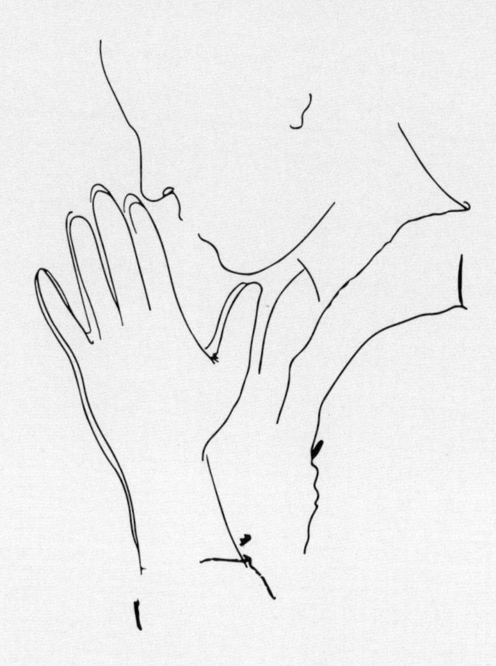

Step 1: To put this into practice, take a quiet moment to acknowledge anything that feels unresolved within you. Close your eyes or lower your gaze. Take a couple of anchoring breaths (see page 18).

Step 2: Then, slowly repeat the forgiveness mantra in full: 'I'm sorry. Please forgive me. Thank you. I love you.'

Step 3: Continue to repeat the mantra until you feel a sense of resolve.

Tip: When you have the space, try reciting this mantra 108 times. The number 108 has been highly revered for thousands of years and holds sacred significance across cultures and religions. It is said that performing a mantra 108 times helps bring you in harmony with the vibrations of the universe.

The Breath of Fire

'Breathe deeply, until sweet air extinguishes the burn of fear in your lungs and every breath is a beautiful refusal to become anything less than infinite.'
– D. Antoinette Foy

We often hold our breath when an uncomfortable emotion arises, but it is breathing that allows that energy to be released. Pranayama is an ancient yogic practice, which translates as 'life force or breath'. The Breath of Fire is a form of pranayama that can be used to ignite the process of letting go. With numerous benefits including detoxification of the body, releasing suppressed emotions and quieting the mind, Breath of Fire is one of the foundational breath techniques used in the practice of Kundalini yoga. Regular practise can reduce stress, boost brain function and improve respiratory health.

The Breath of Fire is rapid, rhythmic and continuous. It is practised as a nasal breath with the mouth closed. Emphasis is placed on the exhale being expelled through the nose by pressing the navel point back and up towards the spine. The inhale that follows is passive and relaxed. Each breath is equal with no pause between. Your chest should stay relaxed and slightly lifted throughout the breathing cycles. There shouldn't be any tension in your shoulders, hands, face or feet.

Step 1: Find a comfortable, seated position and take a couple of conscious breaths to connect.

Step 2: Lengthen through your spine and soften your shoulders away from your ears.

Step 3: Close your eyes or soften your gaze and relax your jaw.

Step 4: Inhale through the nose and focus on your navel.

Step 5: Now exhale sharply through your nose and feel your navel draw back towards your spine. Allow each inhalation to be passive and each exhalation to be a short burst engaging your upper abdomen.

Step 6: Continue breathing like this, finding a steady rhythm.

Step 7: Remove any pause between the passive breath in and the active breath out.

Step 8: Keep the pumping movement in your belly connected with your breath.

Step 9: Practice for up to a minute and notice how you feel.

Tip: If you're exploring this technique for the first time, begin slowly and work up to a faster pace as you get comfortable. Begin with a duration of 1–3 minutes and increase over time, completing multiple repetitions with breaks to breathe naturally in between.

Caution: Avoid this practice if you are pregnant, on your menstrual cycle or have high blood pressure or heart or lung issues.

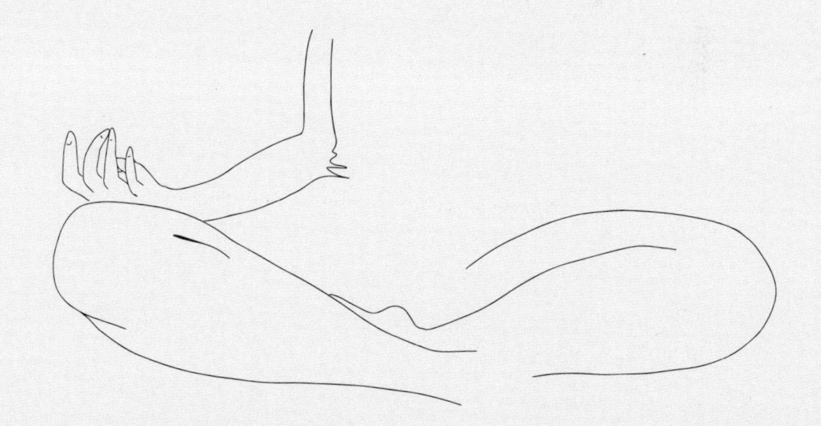

Energy Cleanse

'Your sacred space is where you can find yourself over and over again.'
- Joseph Campbell

Have you ever noticed how much a song can shift your mood? The way everything seems to feel better when the sun comes out? Or how long an unfriendly encounter can linger in your mind (and your body)?

Everything in life is a vibration. As human beings, we are highly susceptible to different frequencies from external influences. Sometimes when we're not feeling ourselves, it's because we have absorbed too much of other people's stuff.

Energy cleansing enables us to rid ourselves of lingering low vibrational frequencies that we have naturally picked up through the day, so we can find ourselves again. Regularly cleansing our body, mind and space removes stagnant energy around us and within us.

Smudging is an ancient practice used to cleanse a person or space by burning medicinal herbs. The herbs are tied into a bundle and dried, before being burned for their sacred smoke. Smudging with sage is commonly known for its potent purifying qualities, but many other herbs can be used, each carrying their own unique healing properties. Eucalyptus is full of healing properties, purifies the air and stimulates the senses. Rosemary is mood-boosting, improves memory and is said to attract good energy. Sage removes bacteria from the air and is said to improve intuition. Lavender boosts happiness and aids a restful night's sleep.

Homemade Smudge Sticks

Creating your own smudge sticks using locally grown herbs is an environmentally friendly alternative to ready-made versions from foreign lands. Avoid using over-harvested herbs.

Step 1: Forage your favourite herbs in your garden or a public community garden.

Step 2: Bundle your chosen herbs together, with the bases of the largest leaves at the same level. Using a length of twine or cotton thread, tie a knot at the bottom of the herb bundle and wrap around to bind the leaves together.

Step 3: Spiral the thread towards the top of the bundle and then back down to the bottom.

Step 4: Tie the loose end of the thread to the original knot at the bottom.

Step 5: Hang your smudge stick upside down and allow 3 weeks to dry.

Energetic Cleanse Checklist

Set an intention

Before you begin your energy cleansing ritual, it's important to have an intention in mind. What do you want to release? What would you like to call in?

Declutter

Are you holding onto any physical items that no longer bring you joy? Is there anything taking up unnecessary space that you can neatly pack away? Keeping your environment clean and clutter-free creates less energetic congestion.

Let the air in

Open your windows and allow fresh air in, refreshing your space and filling it with clean, positive energy. A breath of fresh air is also a great way to channel clarity.

Get salty

Salt is an incredible natural resource for absorbing negative energy. After you've tended to the cleansing of your space, have a relaxing foot soak with a couple of handfuls of sea salt to enhance the cleansing of your body and aura.

No matter what, I will *always* have my own back. What I give to myself, *no one* else can take away.

SELF-
SOOTHE

In moments of overwhelm, when thinking is difficult and solutions feel unclear, sometimes all I can do is wrap my body in the safety of my own arms and tell myself that everything is going to be OK. This is what it means to self-soothe. To calm and comfort ourselves when we're experiencing distress. To move our minds away from unwanted thoughts, feelings and impulses, and offer ourselves an inward kindness when we need it the most. When we move from our heads into our hearts to be with ourselves in that space, we connect to our innermost being with warmth and love, and we become our own medicine.

Self-soothing builds inner resilience and reminds us of our ability to self-regulate. The first step is always to check in and notice what we're feeling, thinking and experiencing. The next step is to know what we can do or say to soothe and support ourselves. Sometimes we require tender compassion, giving ourselves space to heal and permission to rest. Other times we need fierce compassion, ordering ourselves out of a slump with affirming words of kindness and encouragement. When we tend to our innermost longings with attentiveness and care, we can discover our 'love languages'. We can become our own cheerleaders both in moments of difficulty and moments of joy

The most important relationship we have is the one we have with ourselves. So let's make a habit of showing ourselves that we have our own back. In the words of holistic health coach Susan Weiss Berry, 'Every act of self-care is a powerful declaration: I am on my side, I am on my side, each day I am more and more on my own side.'

Pillow Self-Talk

'There are days I drop words of comfort on myself like falling leaves and remember that it is enough to be taken care of by myself.'

– Brian Andreas

Think about pillow talk, that intimate conversation between a romantic couple. In the name of radical self-care, I've reimagined it as an affirmation practice to build self-intimacy. What better time to start a loving dialogue with yourself than first thing in the morning? What better place than from the comfort of your bed while your head still rests on your pillow? This practice invites you to communicate with yourself intimately and openly, to be honest about any feelings you've woken up with and give yourself the love and encouragement you need for the day ahead. The way that you speak to yourself matters. Filling up with affirming words of kindness creates less space for negative thoughts to enter in. It also makes you more aware and less judgemental of recurring thought patterns and feelings. If you share a bed with someone and cannot practice this out loud, have the conversation in your head.

Step 1: Upon waking in the morning, take a moment to acknowledge your energy and mood.

Step 2: Recite the following statement out loud or in your head: 'I choose to be with myself, fully in this moment, to give myself my undivided attention. I accept myself as I am. I accept whatever emotions I am experiencing for what they are'.

Step 3: Now begin to speak affirming words to yourself, focusing on positive language:

'I am...'
'I can...'
'I have...'
'I love...'.

Step 4: Rather than bypassing anything challenging you may be experiencing, meet it with mindfulness and compassion: 'Even though I am experiencing ... I trust that I will get through it.'

Step 5: If past regrets or future worries arise, acknowledge them and bring your focus back to the day ahead. Choose an affirmation below to carry with you.

'Just for today, I choose to meet myself with gentleness and compassion.'
'Just for today, I choose to meet myself with trust and belief.'
'Just for today, I choose to meet myself with patience and hope.'
'Just for today, I choose to meet myself with acceptance and understanding.'
'Just for today, I choose to meet myself with curiosity and openness.'
'Just for today, I choose to meet myself with encouragement and love.'

Step 6: Create a mantra that you can return to and recite for on-the-go encouragement. My personal favourites are:

'All will be well.'
'I am held and supported.'
'I trust in life and I trust in myself.'

Evening Ritual

Pillow talk also works as an evening ritual.

Step 1: Just before you go to sleep at night, take a moment to acknowledge your energy and mood.

Step 2: Now think of something great you achieved during your day and congratulate yourself for it.

Step 3: Acknowledge anything that didn't go your way or that you would have liked to do differently.

Step 4: Remind yourself that tomorrow is a brand-new day and an opportunity to start afresh.

Step 5: Think about three things you are grateful for and feel your heart warm before drifting off to sleep.

Tip: Expressing gratitude has been shown to alter your brain chemistry and benefit your mental health. Ending your day with feelings of gratitude will help send you off to sleep with feel-good hormones circulating, and maybe even with a smile.

Mirror Work

'The most important relationship we can all have is the one you have with yourself.'
– Aristotle

What do you see when you look in the mirror? What do you tell yourself as a result? More often than not, we gaze at our reflection to analyse (and critique) our appearance or to make ourselves more 'presentable' for the outside world. What if we took the time to admire the beauty that radiates from our inner essence and remind ourselves that being who we are is enough? Mirror work is an empowering ritual that invites us to meet our reflection with openness, compassion and self-affirming words. The practice aims to build self-intimacy and improve the relationship we have with ourselves.

Reciting positive affirmations is known to have a positive effect on our self-perception. Looking ourselves in the eyes as we're doing this elevates the effects even more. Over time, mirror work can transform the way you see yourself, encouraging self-love and increased self-confidence. When we face ourselves and embrace our own power, we can meet the outside world with more courage and trust.

Step 1: Stand in front of a mirror in a private space where you will be free from distractions.

Step 2: Acknowledge your thoughts and mood.

Step 3: Take a few anchoring breaths (see page 18) to connect to your body.

Step 4: Make eye contact with yourself in the mirror.

Step 5: Notice what comes to mind and how you feel in your body. Continue to gaze into your own reflection.

Step 6: Acknowledge any feelings of awkwardness or discomfort.

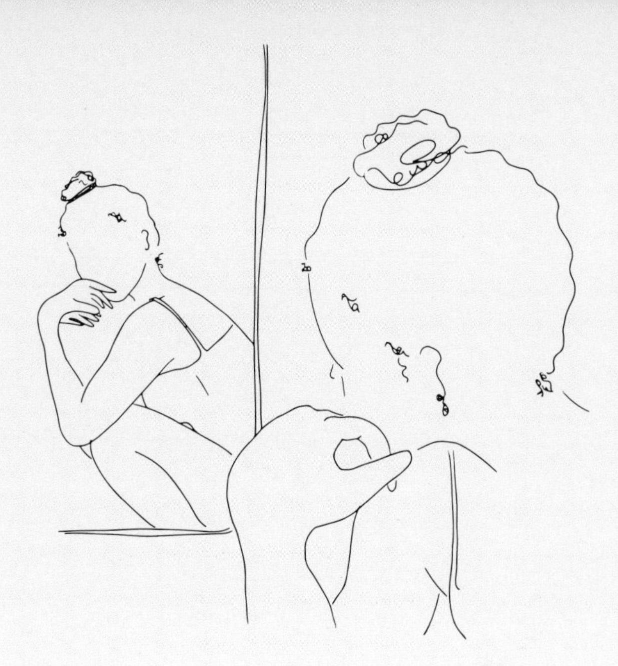

Step 7: Observe whether your gaze is critical and harsh or soft and welcoming. Try to release any judgements and focus on the spark in your eyes.

Step 8: Begin to recite the following affirmations, taking slow conscious breaths throughout and allowing the words to be received:

'I am love.'
'I am light.'
'I am energy.'
'I am divinity wrapped in skin.'
'I am powerful and worthy.'
'I am all that I need.'
'All that is possible is possible for me.'

Step 9: Repeat each affirmation as many times as you like.

Step 10: Finish with a smile and an affectionate breath.

Tip: As you warm into this ritual, create your own affirmations to support your transformation. Think of any specific encouragement you need or any self-limiting beliefs you'd like to shift. Remember to focus on positive language. Practice once a week or daily for maximum benefits. You may not notice a shift right away but stick with it.

Healing Hands

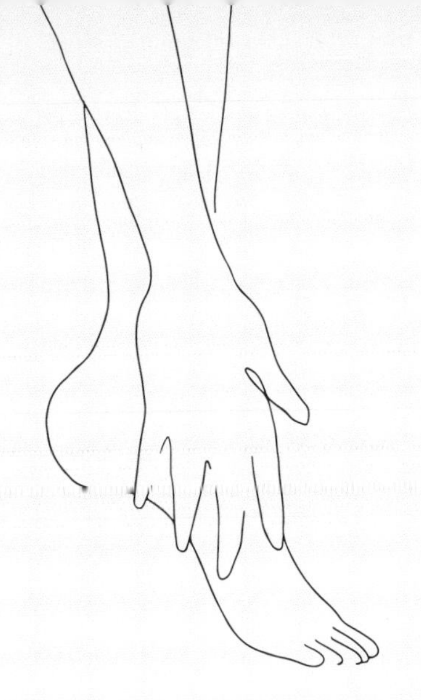

'You yourself, as much as anybody in the entire universe, deserve your love and affection.'
– Buddha

Our hands are an extension of our hearts. When we hold someone close or reach out to offer a gift, we are pouring love through our hands often without even realising it. Our hands are in constant service to the world around us. What if we offered some of that back to ourselves?

Touch is our first language. It soothes us and signals safety and trust. Even the simplest caring touch offered to ourselves can trigger the release of our love hormone, oxytocin. Self-massage takes the benefits of touch even further by relieving stress and achy muscles. It offers direct intimacy with our own bodies and an opportunity to pour love into any areas we may have neglected. Everyone can receive the love and care they so readily give away to others through self-massage. This ritual is inspired by Abhyanga, the Ayurvedic practice of self-massage using warm oil. (Any inexpensive natural oil that feels great on your skin will work well.)

Step 1: Place your bottle of oil in a wash basin or large bowl of hot water to warm it.

Step 2: Test the temperature by putting a drop of the oil on your inner wrist. The oil should be comfortably warm.

Step 3: Before you begin, take a moment to acknowledge your thoughts and mood. Take a couple of anchoring breaths (see page 18) to connect to your body.

Step 4: Start massaging the top of your head and scalp using circular strokes, as if shampooing your hair.

Step 5: Bring your fingers to your forehead and gently massage outwards in circular movements towards your temples.

Step 6: Continue these circular movements around your cheeks and across your jaw always moving upwards and outwards.

Step 7: Take time to massage your ears and earlobes, neck and shoulders.

Step 8: Now move on to your body, using long strokes on your arms and legs, and circular strokes on your elbows and knees. Massage inwardly in the direction of the heart.

Step 9: Use broad, clockwise, circular motions to massage your belly and chest.

Step 10: Now spend a couple of minutes attentively massaging your feet.

Step 11: To finish, take a moment to acknowledge all the love you've poured out through these hands of yours, and wrap your hands lovingly around yourself. Embrace yourself deeply. Enjoy the feeling of having nourished and cared for your body.

Step 12: Rinse any excess oil off and gently blot your skin with a towel, or alternatively, leave the oil to absorb into the skin.

Tip: This ritual is best practiced in a warm room, after a steamy bath or shower. Always do a patch test when using a new product on your skin.

The Humming Effect

'You are just a little bit of relief away from letting a whole lot of good stuff in!'
- Abraham Hicks

Humming and singing can often be unconsciously self-soothing. To simplify the science behind it, humming creates internal vibrations that stimulate our vagus nerve, which is a major contributor to how our body and brain function. This vagus nerve stimulation plays a key role in activating the parasympathetic nervous system, otherwise known as our 'rest and digest' state. Learning this I realised why I randomly hum to myself when feeling cold, nervous, stressed or stuck. One of the best things about humming is that anyone can do it. As well as inducing calmness, humming has been shown to enhance sleep, regulate blood pressure and boost our bodies with the love hormone, oxytocin.

Because it increases the length of an exhalation, humming with deep conscious breathing is a powerful combination. Humming Bee Breath, or Bhramari pranayama, is an ancient yogic breathing technique that utilises sound by humming on the exhalation. The vibrational sound and extended exhalation help to downregulate the nervous system and create calm. In Sanskrit, *bhramari* means 'big black bee', which is fitting as the sound created is like that of a buzzing bee.

Step 1: Find a comfortable, seated position and take a couple of conscious breaths to connect.

Step 2: Lengthen through your spine and soften your shoulders away from your ears.

Step 3: Close your eyes or soften your gaze.

Step 4: Raise your hands towards your ears keeping your elbows level with your shoulders.

Step 5: Plug your ears with your index fingers, keeping your shoulders relaxed.

Step 6: Inhale deeply through your nose, drawing the breath up from your belly to the top of your chest.

Step 7: Begin to hum the breath out with an 'Mmmmmm' sound all the way to the end of your exhalation.

Step 8: Repeat this cycle for 6–8 rounds, feeling the vibrations within.

Step 9: When you have completed the final round, release your arms and place your hands on your thighs, palms facing the ceiling.

Step 10: Feel the vibrations of your last hum echo throughout your body.

Tip: For a deeper experience, cover your eyes with your fingers and block your ears with your thumbs.

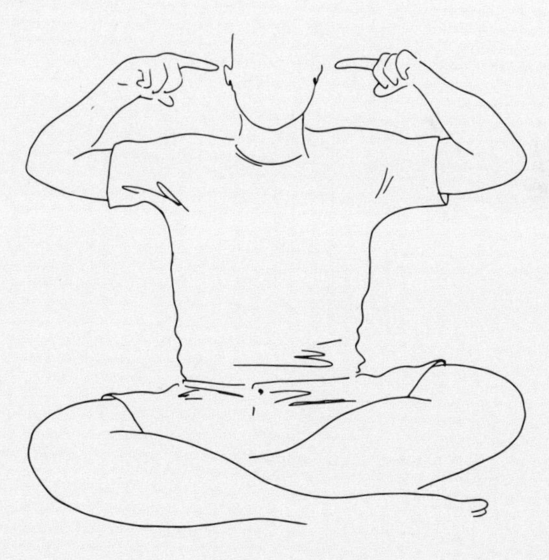

Dear Self

'Talk to yourself like someone you love.'
- Brené Brown

It was the last day of a month-long yoga practitioner training with The Sacred Fig. As I rested following our final movement practice, I sensed that a gift of some kind had been placed close by. Sure enough, when I sat up, there beside me was a piece of folded paper with my name on it. Eagerly I opened it up and began to read what I felt were the most beautiful loving words ever written. Tears streamed down my cheeks as I realised these adoring words were written by me. On the very first day, we'd been invited to write ourselves a letter and place it in a bowl. I'd totally forgotten about the letter until that moment four weeks later. It was one of the most precious gifts I've received. This ritual is inspired by that experience.

You'll need a pen and paper or a journal. You can write to yourself anywhere, as long as you are able to be fully present with the practice. If you are at home, it may help to have a soothing playlist to set the mood. If you're out and about, find a bench to perch on or a tree to sit under.

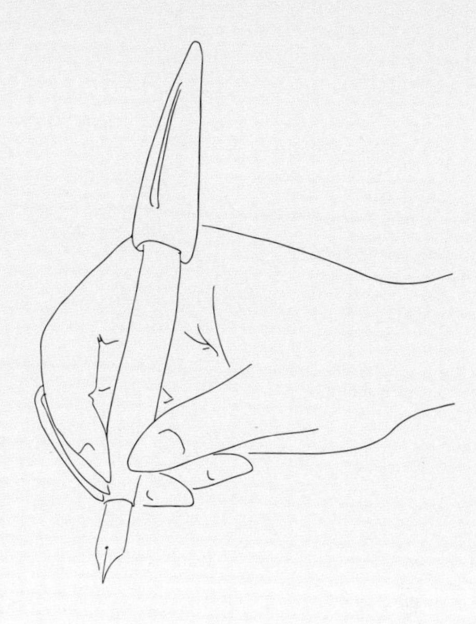

Step 1: Wherever you are, take a few anchoring breaths (see page 18) to connect to your body.

Step 2: Now pick up your pen and begin to write, 'Dear Self…'. Allow words of loving kindness to pour out onto the paper. Be gentle with yourself. Be open. If you struggle to get started think of how you would encourage and uplift your dearest friend.

Step 3: Don't think too much about making sense, but rather focus on the feeling of the words that flow from your pen. Your love letter can be as long as you want. A few paragraphs or a few pages.

Step 4: When you're finished, sign off 'Love…' and your name.

Use this ritual as an opportunity to express the love and gratitude you have for yourself as often as you can. Remind yourself how capable you are and how far you have come. Resist the temptation to read over the words straight away. Just fold up the paper and place the letter somewhere you can stumble across it in the future.

I am capable of balancing *ease* and *effort* in my life. I allow myself to *relax* and *recharge*. My brilliance arises from conscious rest.

CONSCIOUS REST

Beyond the need to grow, evolve and develop, we need to rest. I'm not just talking about the sleep we get at night. Sleep optimisation has many health benefits, like stress reduction, mood regulation and immune system support. But it's important to note that this isn't the only type of rest we need to feel well. Rest is anything that makes our nervous system feel safe enough for stress responses to switch off.

Rest can be found in simplifying our schedules. It can be time spent away from the overstimulation of our screens or saying no to energy-depleting activities. It can be found in taking a break from striving and overthinking to focus on the present moment. Of course, the hours of sleep we get at night count. But rest can also consist of a walk in nature, a few minutes spent in a restorative yoga pose, an afternoon siesta or even a single conscious breath.

With demands on our time and attention at an all-time high, being busy can often feel more familiar than taking time out. Rebelling against burnout-inducing busyness means reconnecting to the body and honouring its call for downtime, prioritising more restfulness and ease during the day. When we can't completely switch off, we can try to slow down, and find different ways to rest the body and mind, as often as we can. Radical rest is self-preservation. Rest loudly and proudly and give others permission to do the same.

Upside-Down Pose

'It's precisely those who are busiest who most need to give themselves a break.'
- Pico Iyer

A restorative ritual to aid the dulling effects of a long, stressful day is to get upside down. Inversions are a type of yoga pose where the body is sometimes quite literally turned on its head. These poses improve blood circulation and lymphatic drainage, which can relieve heaviness and tension, and rebalance fluids, blood flow and energy. They also have a calming and relaxing effect on the mind. There are several ways to practise being upside down, the safest and most gentle being Legs Up The Wall pose, or Viparita Karani in Sanskrit. In ancient yogic tradition, this pose was said to reverse signs of ageing. While I can't promise that, just a few minutes of rest in this pose should allow you to return to your day feeling calmer and refreshed.

Step 1: Find a wall or another surface where you can prop up your legs.

Step 2: Lay on your side at a right angle to the wall or surface with your bottom and legs as close to the wall or surface as possible.

Step 3: Roll over onto your back and stretch your legs up towards the ceiling, bringing them to rest on the wall (or whatever you are using to prop them up).

Step 4: Take a moment to settle into the pose, finding a position that feels good for your body.

Step 5: Now release all effort, breathe and relax for 5–10 minutes.

Step 6: When you are ready to come out of the pose, bend your legs and gently roll back onto your side, taking a few deep breaths here before slowly pushing yourself back upright and easing back into your day.

Tip: Turn up the comfort level in this pose by placing a folded blanket or small cushion beneath your lower back and rolling up a small towel to create an eye pillow to place over your eyes.

Caution: Avoid this practice if you are pregnant, menstruating, or experiencing heart conditions. You could instead try a variation of Corpse pose, or Savasana, with your legs only slightly elevated. To do this, lie flat on your back and place a bolster or folded blankets underneath your feet and knees.

The Ragdoll

'Take a deep breath. Inhale peace.
Exhale happiness.'
- A.D. Posey

Overactive minds can benefit from the rest and reset qualities of the Ragdoll. Known also as Dangling pose, this variation of a standing forward bend releases the lower back while revitalising the mind. The Ragdoll is one of my go-to practices when I am working on something and get stuck, as it provides a way to give myself a reset. Forward bends encourage a mild increase in blood pressure towards the head. This can have a profoundly calming effect on the nervous system and brain. As a result, practising these bends can relieve stress and anxiety, promoting relaxation and mental clarity.

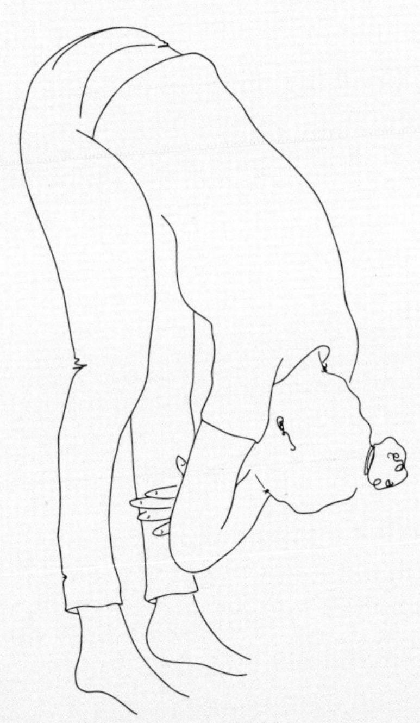

Step 1: Begin standing with the feet hip distance apart.

Step 2: Check that your knees point straight ahead and that your thighs are parallel.

Step 3: Bend your knees slightly, take a deep inhale and, as you exhale, bend at the hips, allowing your upper body to fall over your legs.

Step 4: Release your head and neck and allow your arms to hang heavy.

Step 5: Slowly shift your body weight slightly forwards to feel a stretch down the backs of your legs. If you have tight hamstrings, keep your knees bent to avoid straining your lower back.

Step 6: Either relax in this position or slowly sway from side to side.

Step 7: Breathe deeply to help release tension in your head and upper body.

Step 8: Now cross your arms and softly grasp each elbow with the opposite hand.

Step 9: Relax here or continue to sway from side to side.

Step 10: Stay in this pose for 3–5 deep conscious breaths, in and out through the nose.

Step 11: To come out of the pose, slowly roll back up to standing upright, starting low in your spine and letting your head come up last.

Step 12: Take a moment to stand tall and still, and to acknowledge any mental or physical shifts.

Tip: If you feel a lot of pressure in your lower back, rest your hands on a small stool or stack of books to support the weight of your upper body.

Caution: Avoid this practice if you are pregnant or have a back or neck injury.

Dreamer's Pose

'Each of us needs to withdraw from the cares which will not withdraw from us.'

– Maya Angelou

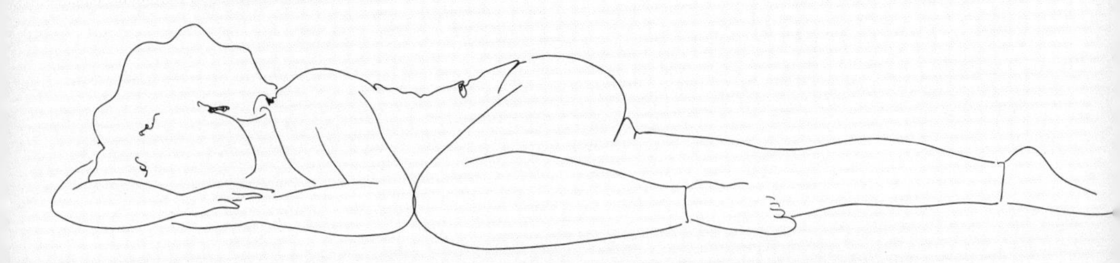

One of my favourite positions to rest in is Matsya Kridasana. In Hatha yoga, it's also known as Flapping Fish, a restorative pose for rest and relaxation. It's said to resemble the shape of a playing fish, flapping its tail and fins in the water. I call it the Dreamer's pose because it is often the position I'm in when I fall asleep. Spending time in this pose creates a restorative passive stretch with a deeply calming effect. As far as yoga postures go, it has very few contra-indications and can be practised by almost everyone. It relaxes and releases tight muscles while gently lengthening the side abdominals, lower back and hips. Enjoy this pose for conscious rest at any time you have a few minutes to lay down, or just before you go to sleep at night. For more comfort, use a pillow or folded blanket to support the parts of your body that come in contact with the ground.

Step 1: Create a comfortable area to lie down on the floor, using extra blankets and cushions for additional padding.

Step 2: Lie down on your belly.

Step 3: Turn your head to the left and place your right cheek on the floor.

Step 4: Place your left foot towards your right knee. Make sure it touches for the entire duration of the pose.

Step 5: Place your arms on the floor over your head, palms down, with the tips of your middle fingers touching. Then twist your upper body to the left to bring your left elbow towards your left knee.

Step 6: Adjust your position to feel comfortable and grounded.

Step 7: Relax here, taking long, deep breaths and closing your eyes if you like. Keep your awareness of your breath and note how it feels within your body.

Step 8: Let your thoughts become weightless, coming and going like clouds in the sky.

Step 9: Stay here for as long as you wish and then switch to the other side.

Step 10: To release, gently open your eyes, straighten your body and press up to a seated position. Take another minute or so here before standing up.

Noble Silence

'Listen to silence. It has so much to say.'
– Rumi

Peace and quiet invite us to rest. Traditionally a Buddhist practice, Noble Silence will help quiet the mind and encourage mindful speech. It can be a tool for deep transformation. Bringing awareness to our inner voice deepens our connection with ourselves. During my yoga teacher training with The Sacred fig, we were invited to observe silence each morning. This meant refraining from any form of communication, whether by speech, gesture, physical touch or eye contact. To wake up in the same room and not greet the person beside me was strange at first. But as the days passed, it began to feel like a gift to have that sacred time alone with my thoughts and feelings. It made me aware of how much energy is consumed communicating with others in our daily lives – and how exhausting that can be without taking conscious breaks from it.

Every day, family and work life require lots of external communication, but in learning to refrain from speaking every word we think, we become more intentional about what we share. We conserve more of our energy and are better resourced during times when communicating well is most important. Here are some ideas for weaving noble silence throughout a busy day.

In the morning

Wake up early enough to have at least 11 minutes of undisturbed silent meditation. Use this time to carefully observe your mood and energy. Rest in the silence between your thoughts.

During the day

Slow down your speech when communicating with others. Be less reactive in your replies. Take time to feel into what you'd like to share before you share it. Allow for more silence between words and sentences.

In the evening

Put your phone on silent mode two hours before you go to sleep. Choose an activity that you can practice quietly, whether it is reading, drawing or journaling about your day.

At first, it may feel difficult or even impossible to observe silence every day, but the more you do, the more spaciousness you'll create. Be sure to let those you live and work with know so they can support your practice.

Saying No

'When you say "yes" to others, make sure you are not saying "no" to yourself.'
- Paulo Coelho

As a people pleaser in recovery, the practice of saying no is still something I contend with. I often jump at opportunities to say yes because I enjoy being helpful. Before I know it, I've said yes to more than I can manage, and I'm left feeling overwhelmed and anxious about letting anyone down. The hard truth I'm still learning is that taking care of myself will sometimes mean letting others down. The alternative is continuously abandoning my needs to please others and, at worst, making myself sick. Sure, it feels great to please other people and be generous with the time and energy we give out - but this cannot be at the expense of our health. The desire to take care of ourselves must be greater than our desire to please others. We need to prioritise filling our own cups so that we can then pour into others from a resourced and empowered place. Here is a guide to decision-making that was introduced to me by dear friend and happiness psychologist Anya Pearse. When considering whether to accept or decline an invitation, practise R.I.S.E.

R – Register how I feel.

I – Consider what 'I' need right now and how I am tending to that.

S – Stand on your sacred ground with integrity and authenticity.

E – Express your boundaries with clarity and compassion.

Saying no is a practice. It takes courage and commitment. It means slowing down our normal inclination to say yes and feeling what we truly want and need. Our time isn't infinite and there is only so much we can say yes to. Saying no not only creates more space for rest, but it also means more opportunities to do what is truly important and show up more fully for those opportunities that are most meaningful to you. Remember you can be soft in your heart and firm in your boundaries.

A few ways you can politely decline an invitation while being honest and direct is to employ these responses.

'Thanks, but that doesn't work for me.'
'That doesn't feel good in my body.'
'I don't have the capacity right now.'
'No, but thank you for thinking of me.'

I am nature and nature is me. I am part of the great tapestry of life, *interconnected* with all that exists.

NATURE'S GIFTS

Connecting with nature is one of the most powerful support tools for building inner resilience. Nature soothes and restores, calms and regulates. It is radical self-care at its finest, as it provides an abundance of wellbeing benefits and doesn't cost a thing! Research has shown that spending time in nature can enhance memory and focus, relieve stress and anxiety, and even balance blood pressure. When life gets tough, nature also gives us a sense of perspective, reminding us that there is always a bigger picture and bigger forces at play. For many of us living in urban environments, time spent in nature gives us a break from the hyper-stimulation we experience during the day. However, we don't need to journey to the countryside to benefit from the medicine nature provides. The gifts of nature are literally everywhere around us.

Deepening our awareness of the natural world invites us to connect deeper with our internal landscapes. It allows us to tap into the primal wisdom and energetic rhymes of life. Nature itself is inherently resilient, in constant flux, ever-changing and adapting. When we connect with nature, we tap into this resilience within ourselves. We learn to embrace life's challenges as an opportunity for growth and expansion. Within this chapter, you will find rituals you can practise to connect with nature's gifts, whether your days are spent sitting in an office building, standing in the middle of a field or anywhere in between.

The Sun
Element: Fire
Qualities: Purifies, charges, warms, illuminates

The Moon
Element: Water
Qualities: Shifts, nourishes, heals, restores

The Land
Element: Earth
Qualities: Grounds, balances, nurtures, stabilises

The Breeze
Element: Air
Qualities: Communicates, liberates, inspires

The Universe
Element: Ether
Qualities: Intuits, imagines, expands

Earthing

'And forget not that the Earth delights to feel your bare feet and the wind longs to play with your hair.'
- Kahlil Gibran

The ground that we walk on is charged with natural healing energy. When connected to this energy, our bodies enter a healing state. The earth's natural electric charge restores and rejuvenates our energy field. It stabilises our physiology at the deepest levels. Earthing has been shown to reduce inflammation, pain and stress, improve blood flow, energy and sleep, and generate a greater sense of wellbeing. Here are some earthing rituals that focus on reconnecting your energy with the earth through direct or indirect contact.

In the grass

Connecting your bare feet to the ground allows you to directly absorb the free-flowing electrons from the earth's surface. Find ways to get your bare feet in the grass as often as possible and pay attention to the feeling of the land beneath them.

On the ground

Lie down flat on a patch of grass in a garden or park and observe the world from this position. Feel how solid the ground is below you. As you breathe deeply, imagine roots travelling from your back into the soil and towards the earth's core.

Grounding indoors

When going outside is not an option, ground yourself indoors. Lie flat on your back, bending your knees if necessary for extra comfort. Invite your body to be received by the floor beneath you. As you breathe deeply, imagine that the earth is rising up to meet you where you are. Allow yourself to be fully held and supported.

Air Bathing

'The breeze at dawn has secrets to tell you.
Don't go back to sleep.' - Rumi

How often do you allow your body to breathe? To let the outdoor air dance on your skin? We are constantly wrapped in clothing, often fully undressing only to take a shower or bath – or to jump into bed. Being covered up all the time can inhibit our skin's natural need to breathe. Fresh air exposure is great for our bodies. It helps to clear our lungs and replenish our cells with a fresh stream of oxygen. Taking deep conscious breaths of fresh air helps to settle our nervous system and brings us into a state of active peacefulness. It's stimulating both physically and emotionally, enabling us to wake up and begin our day feeling alert and revitalised. Incorporate a couple of minutes of air bathing into your morning routine to set you up for a calmer day ahead:

Step 1: Remove your clothes and cover up with a robe or blanket.

Step 2: Open a window and sit by it, keeping the curtains closed for privacy if you're in view of neighbours or passers-by.

Step 3: Breathe deeply, filling your lungs with fresh oxygenated air. Observe how the air feels as it enters your body.

Step 4: Feel your body relax as you breathe out.

Step 5: Without fully removing your robe or blanket, allow different parts of your body to feel the breeze flowing in, starting with your face, shoulders and neck.

Step 6: Then expose your arms and hands and feel the air in those areas.

Step 7: If privacy allows, remove your blanket or robe completely.

Step 8: Feel the fresh breeze dance across your skin. Carry this sense of refreshed radiance into the rest of your day.

Rise with the Sun

'Every morning, the rising sun invites and inspires us to begin again.'
- Debasish Mridha

When you need a reminder of the miracle that we're living in, follow the sunrise. It is one of the most beautiful natural phenomena on this planet, available to most of us every single morning. Rising with the sun helps to regulate our body's internal clock, keeping us more alert during the day and supporting our sleep cycle at night. Studies have shown that watching the sun rise (or set) can ease stress, boost our mood and ignite our creativity. Just a moment basking in sunlight can transform the way that we feel, expand our awareness and transport us into a deeply meditative state.

Step 1: A good morning starts from the evening before, so prepare yourself with a reasonable bedtime. Before putting your phone on airplane mode, set a gentle alarm to wake you up in time to catch the sun rise. Consider where you can be best positioned to see the sun come up from the east.

Step 2: Upon waking up, stretch your body in a way that feels most pleasing to you. Then make something warm to drink and head towards your chosen location in time to greet the sun. You can observe the sky through a window, but where possible, go outside.

Step 3: Avoid looking directly into the sun as it rises. Instead, gaze towards the light beams that begin to fill the sky. Observe the tapestry of colours.

Step 4: Close your eyes and notice if you can feel the sun's warmth on your face. Imagine golden light from the sun pouring into your heart, filling you with radiance. Notice any tingling sensations or emotions that arise as you breathe deeply into this energetic exchange.

Step 5: Give thanks to the sun for its abundance of warmth and life-giving energy. Carry the radiance you received into the rest of your day.

Tip: If you struggle to wake up early enough for sunrise, modify this ritual for sunset instead.

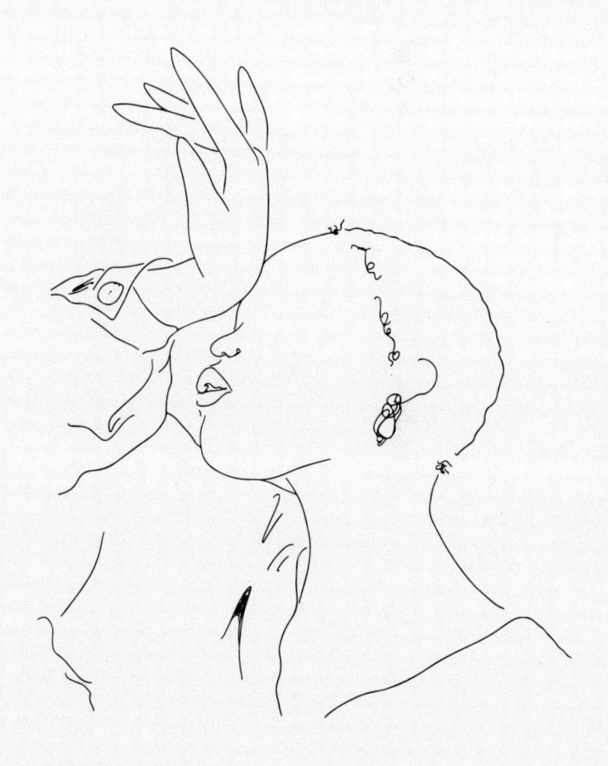

Seasonal Shifts

'Life is a series of natural and spontaneous changes.'
– Lao Tzu

The natural world is always growing and evolving in a state of constant change within a series of infinite patterns. Attuning to Mother Nature's seasonal shifts is a great way to remind ourselves of our own cyclical nature; it invites us to ebb and flow with life rather than against it.

In ancient times, following nature's cycles was a normal way of being; living in connection with the land and following the seasons, rising with the sun and resting as it sets. Nowadays of course, things look a lot different. While we cannot completely reject the modern world, finding ways to return to nature's rhythms has widespread benefits, including better mental and physical health, increased productivity and awareness, self-acceptance, reconnection to our intuitive nature and an increased sense of interconnection.

The seasonal cycle of the year is created by earth's annual orbit around the sun. You can adjust the way that you eat, sleep, work and play following the season you are in and the energy that season requires. For example, allowing yourself to rest more during the darker autumn and winter months helps prepare you for the upward expansive energy that spring and summer bring. Get to know the qualities of each season and how you relate to them mentally, emotionally, physically and energetically.

Solstices are the extreme points as earth's axis tilts towards or away from the sun when days and nights are longest or shortest. On equinoxes, days and nights are equal in all parts of the world. Mark these days in your calendar to honour seasonal shifts with focused reflection and ritual.

The Spring Equinox: Renewal and Rebirth

Ritual: Write a list of what you'd like to feel and experience over the next six months. Plant the paper in the earth, symbolising trust that your intentions will soon blossom and be realised.

Journal prompt: Where can I clear space for fresh energy to come in and revitalise me?

Affirmation: 'I am open to new perspectives and growth.'

Summer Solstice: Joy and Abundance

Ritual: Watch the sun both rise and set on the longest day of the year to acknowledge its life-giving power.

Journal prompts: What lights me up? When do I feel most creative, playful and alive?

Affirmation: 'My energy is warm and bright, like sunshine.'

The Autumn Equinox: Shedding and Letting Go

Ritual: Write a list of all that you have achieved through the summer months. Carefully reflect on and consider what you are grateful for and what you are ready to let go of.

Journal prompts: What did I learn about myself in the last three months? What am I ready to release?

Affirmation: 'I embrace my emotions and I nurture my instincts.'

Winter Solstice: Contemplation and Rest

Ritual: Create an altar with items that bring you joy and peace. Light candles around the objects as a symbol of the sun's ability to give us life and light on the darkest of days.

Journal prompts: What did I discover about myself this year? What feels more important than ever?

Affirmation: 'I honour my body's cues to rest and refuel.'

Lunar Energy

'Don't worry if you're making waves just by being yourself. The Moon does it all the time.'
- Scott Stabile

From new to full and back again, the lunar cycle is a powerful symbol of transformation and renewal. Our ocean tides are influenced by the moon's gravitational pull, and as beings made up of mostly water, it only makes sense that we are impacted too. Moving with the moon invites us to become more observant of our own emotional tides and attune to the potent energies of the lunar pulse. The entire moon cycle unfolds over approximately 29.5 days, a period commonly referred to as a lunar month. Each phase of the moon brings with it a unique opportunity for growth and introspection.

New Moon

This first phase of the lunar cycle, also known as the dark moon, is entirely in shadow. The energy of the new moon supports fresh starts and beginnings, inviting you to embrace new paths and possibilities. It's a great period for setting intentions and planting metaphorical seeds for the future.

Ritual: Modify the Daily Desires practice on page 54 to map out what you want the month ahead to feel like.

Journal prompt: What new beginnings am I ready to embrace?

Waxing Moon

The second and first visible phase appears as a thin crescent on the right side of the moon. The energy of the waxing moon supports growth, intention and magnetism. Now is the time to take steps towards the intentions you set during the new moon phase.

Ritual: Revisit what you would like your month to feel like and think about the small steps you can take today towards the bigger vision you have for yourself.

Journal prompt: How can I support myself in this growth process?

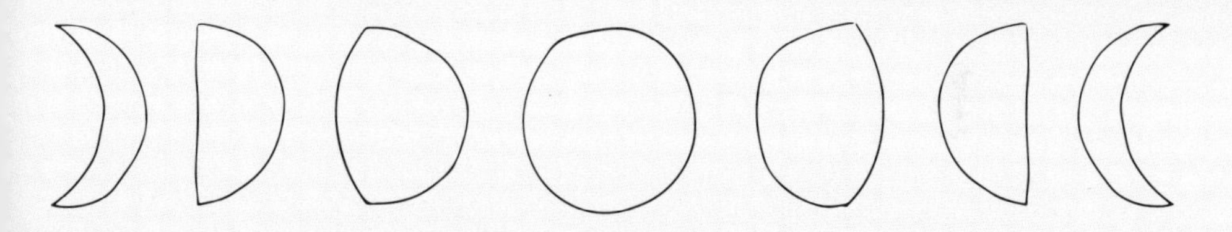

First Quarter Moon

In the third phase of the lunar cycle, half of the right side of the moon is illuminated. This is the halfway point between the new moon and the full moon. The energy of the first quarter moon supports actions, decisions and commitments. It's the perfect time to assess your previous intentions and decide what needs to be revised.

Ritual: Reflect on your progress so far and think about any adjustments you wish to make.

Journal prompt: What aligned actions are needed for me to move closer to my dreams?

Waxing Gibbous Moon

Illumination of the moon continues to grow during the fourth phase, covering the right side of the moon's surface. The energy of the waxing gibbous moon supports refinement and fine-tuning. During this period, focus on the finer details of your goals and make necessary adjustments, aligning closer to your intentions with patience and persistence.

Ritual: Review your progress again and refine your intentions.

Journal prompt: What still needs to be refined or adjusted?

Full Moon

The entire face of the moon is illuminated during the fifth phase, forming a big bright circle in the sky. Thought to be the most powerful phase of the lunar cycle, full moon energy supports deep introspection and big emotional release. It's a great time to celebrate you and focus on the things that are most important in your life.

Ritual: Do something simple that brings you joy and nurtures your inner child.

Journal prompt: What am I most grateful for?

Waning Moon

The moon starts to shrink during phase six, as the illumination decreases on the right side beginning the moon's transition back to darkness. The energy of the waning moon supports cleansing and closure.

Ritual: Create a symbolic act of release, using any of the rituals within the Letting Go chapter (see pages 60–75).

Journal prompt: What am I ready to let go of? How can I express gratitude for what I'm leaving behind?

Third Quarter Moon

In the seventh phase of the lunar cycle, half of the moon is illuminated again, forming the mirror image of the first quarter moon. The energy of the third quarter moon supports overcoming obstacles and releasing any remaining burdens. It's a great time to think about what you would like to rebuild or dismantle in your life to make the process flow with more ease as you prepare for a new beginning.

Ritual: Use the forgiveness mantra on page 68 to release any lingering resentments, frustrations or regrets. Follow with the cleansing energy ritual on page 74.

Journal prompts: What am I ready to release? How can I forgive and move forwards?

Waning Crescent

The moon continues to shrink during the eighth phase, leaving a thin silver crescent on the left side. It's the last visible phase before returning to the new moon. As we circle back to the dark moon phase, focus on getting rid of anything that has been absorbing joy from your life or draining your energy. It's a time of surrender, rest and healing. It's a period to fully let go and prepare for the new cycle ahead.

Ritual: Engage in restorative movement, like the groundwork practice on page 44.

Journal prompt: How can I nurture myself in preparation for a new beginning?

Tip: To further enhance your lunar rituals and reflections, investigate the zodiac sign the moon lands on through each phase. This adds another layer of connection and can highlight different areas in your life to focus attention.

I *honour* the space
in others where the
entire universe resides.
When we *share*
that space together,
we are *one*.

TOGETHERNESS

In the mission to reclaim what it means to take care of ourselves, we must not lose sight of caring for and nurturing each other. We crave connection because we're social beings. Our longing to be part of something bigger than ourselves stems from our tribal roots. We all have needs that cannot be met on our own and resources to share that can support those around us. Togetherness is key to our survival. Contributing to our communities and being open to receiving help when we need it creates an ecosystem of care that everyone can benefit from.

Community can mean different things to different people, but at its core, it's a shared connection to another/others with reciprocal support. This can be friends, family, work colleagues, neighbours, people in your local area or people you connect with online. Engaging with your community can be as simple as offering someone help or asking for a shoulder to cry on. It can be calling out injustices or using your privilege and power towards positive change. Anything that cultivates togetherness is essential for our individual and collective wellbeing.

In caring for our communities, we must acknowledge that every human being should be seen, heard and recognised for who they are. And that we all deserve to be valued, loved and given the chance to live a life of hope, freedom and fairness. It's the support we offer one another that carries us through. Sharing our stories, our fears, our grief and our joy reminds us that we don't need to go it alone.

> *'I'm not sure if resilience is ever achieved alone. Experience allows us to learn from example. But if we have someone who loves us – I don't mean who indulges us, but who loves us enough to be on our side – then it's easier to grow resilience, to grow belief in self, to grow self-esteem. And it's self-esteem that allows a person to stand up.'*
> – Maya Angelou, 'Handle with Care: A Conversation with Maya Angelou', *EL Magazine*, 2013

Finding Your Tribes

'One of the most vital ways we sustain ourselves is by building communities of resistance, places where we know we are not alone.'

– bell hooks

Even in a room full of people, we can still experience feelings of isolation. That's why building positive relationships and connecting with others who share our values, beliefs and desires is so important. It gives us a sense of belonging and purpose. We feel understood, we feel seen and acknowledged for who we are. Some of us may find a single person or group to fulfil our sense of belonging, but most of us will need to diversify and be part of several communities. We are multi-faceted beings with varying needs and varying ways we can contribute.

Think about your existing relationships or groups, and whether there are opportunities to be more honest about what you need or want to contribute. Consider ways to make meaningful connections with people outside of your immediate circles, like joining a group that aligns with your interests or visiting the places you love and seeing who else shows up.

Restoring existing connections and making new ones can feel daunting. The fear of rejection can be crippling, but finding our tribes builds our confidence, increases our resilience and opens us up to new opportunities and experiences. Always remember that any rejection is simply a redirection towards what is really meant for you. Here is a guide to making meaningful connections.

Be authentic

Most of us desperately want to fit in and alter the way we present ourselves to be more accepted. But building genuine connections requires us to show up in the truth of who we are.

Invite depth

Meaningful connections require shared vulnerability. Once trust is established, don't be afraid to dive into more intimate conversations. Move past surface-level talk, or what a friend of mine refers to as 'bus-stop chat'.

Be present

When spending time with your loved ones or someone new you are connecting with, try to be fully there. Put your phone away, leave distractions behind you and give them the gift of your presence.

Set and respect boundaries

Openly communicate your boundaries with the people in your life. Don't be afraid to say no when you need to. Encourage others to do the same. Honour and respect them when they do.

As you continue to grow and evolve, you may leave a community or relationship to join another that better aligns with you. Communicate with openness and compassion. Acknowledge any grief that comes up. Leave well by honouring how much that space or relationship meant to you.

Deep Listening

'People leave traces of themselves where they feel most comfortable, most worthwhile.'

- Haruki Murakami

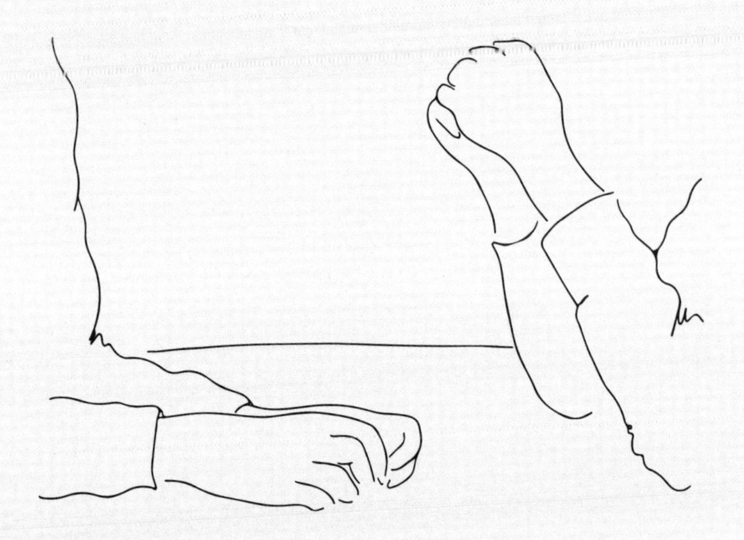

Being fully present with another is a gift. It invites that person to be who they are and encourages meaningful conversation. Deep listening is the practice of embodied presence while another person is talking, which creates a safe space for them to speak their truth and gives them your undivided attention as they share. The more we practice listening to understand rather than listening to respond, the more opportunities we create for authentic connection and shared vulnerability.

Set the scene

Be mindful of where you are and consider if it's a suitable environment for a meaningful conversation to take place. Where possible opt for somewhere quiet that feels safe enough for vulnerable words to be shared. Put your phones on silent to limit distractions.

Give your full attention

Place your full focus on the person sharing. While you are listening, your attention may drift. Notice when this happens and bring your attention back to the conversation. Use anchoring breaths (see page 18) to ground you in the present moment.

Listen with your heart

Listen with kindness and without over-analysing their words. Try not to take anything personally and practise non-judgement with the words you are hearing. Avoid the need to fix, save, advise or correct the other person as they share.

Listen with your eyes

Looking into the eyes of someone sharing is a sign of attentiveness. It lets them know that you are genuinely engaging with what is being expressed.

Seek to understand

Remain curious and open-minded about what is being shared. Seek to understand their point of view. Attempt to understand the meaning behind and in between the words. View the conversation as a journey of discovery.

Respond from the heart

Avoid the temptation to fill empty spaces between the other person's words just for the sake of it. Occasional mindful questions are a great way to invite the conversation to delve deeper. Remember that any heart-led response should reveal the depth of your listening.

Listening to someone with the intent to understand what is being said inspires a true and authentic connection. It can be practised both to make new friends and deepen existing relationships. It's also a great way to find meaningful moments with anyone you encounter during your day.

Acts of Kindness

'Remember there is no such thing as a small act of kindness. Every act creates a ripple with no logical end.'

- Scott Adams

Sharing kindness is contagious. It boosts feelings of happiness and optimism, both in the person giving kindness and the person receiving it. Even someone who witnesses kindness in action receives a feel-good experience. When we are kind to ourselves, we inspire others to meet themselves with compassion. Even the simplest gesture of care can have transformative effects that ripple way beyond the gesture itself.

I once read that Benjamin Franklin would ask himself each morning, 'What good shall I do this day?' Acts of kindness are the small, thoughtful things we can easily incorporate into our existing routines - intentional actions that are motivated by genuine warm feelings. Doing something nice for ourselves or others doesn't need to cost a lot of time or money. It's the small but significant things in life that can make a massive difference.

25 ideas for weaving kindness into every day

1. Smile at the next person you see.
2. Write someone a love note.
3. Call a friend that you haven't spoken to for a while.
4. Tell someone you know that you are proud of them.
5. Tell someone you are thankful for them.
6. Send a motivational text to a friend who is struggling.
7. Send someone you know a joke to cheer them up.
8. Engage in conversation with a shop assistant when paying at the till.
9. Have a clear-out and take items to a charity shop.
10. Make and send a care package to someone who needs it.
11. Let someone jump the queue at the supermarket.
12. Help someone who is lost with directions.
13. Have a conversation with someone who is experiencing homelessness.
14. Pick up rubbish in the street.
15. Donate a book to your nearest library.
16. Write down words of encouragement and leave them in places for people to find.
17. Donate towels or blankets to a shelter.
18. Lend someone your favourite book.
19. Praise a local business online.
20. Share a favourite memory with a loved one.
21. Pass on a good book when you're finished with it.
22. Take a minute to help someone, even if you're in a rush.
23. Give someone a compliment.
24. Say thank you more.
25. Wish a passer-by a good morning or afternoon.

Acts of kindness contribute to a positive community and a better world for everyone. However, being kind to ourselves is just as important as being kind to others. Be mindful of giving too much of yourself or giving beyond your means. Leave enough for you.

Soul Gazing

'The best conversations happen between the eyes.'
- We Are Formless

Soul gazing is a tantric technique used to encourage a deeper level of connection between two people. It involves looking into each other's eyes, in silence, for an extended length of time. Although originally intended for romantic partners, it's a powerful bonding method that you can use with a friend or family member. You may notice the urge to giggle or look away. You may experience feelings of discomfort, awkwardness and fear. This is all okay. The purpose is to move beyond our human insecurities into a higher state of connection to ourselves and the other.

Step 1: Sit face to face, at a comfortable distance, yet close enough to observe each other's eyes.

Step 2: Set a timer for the desired length of time (start with 2–5 minutes and increase with practise).

Step 3: Allow your gaze to meet each other's eyes and let it relax there. Sometimes it's easier to focus on one eye at a time.

Step 4: Relax the body, breathe naturally and allow yourself to blink.

Step 5: Observe feelings that arise and meet them with your breath.

Step 6: When the timer goes off, gently break your gaze and close your eyes. Then open them and return to share your experience.

Tip: Taking a few minutes before you begin to ground yourselves and calm your energies with meditation or slowing down your breath will help relax you into the practice.

Back to Back

'Invisible threads are the strongest ties.'
- Friedrich Nietzsche

Something magic happens when groups come together to meditate. A collective stillness that reverberates beyond bodies. Meditating with just one other person can catalyse feelings of peace, tranquillity and interconnection. This tantra-inspired technique involves sitting with your back against a partner and sharing a meditative breath practice. Breathing in sync invites your awareness to expand beyond your own body. Sitting back-to-back provides a safe and comfortable way of giving and receiving loving contact.

Step 1: Begin sitting back to back with your partner, keeping a few inches of space between you. Take a moment to acknowledge your own energy and mood.

Step 2: Complete a few anchoring breaths (see page 18) to drop your awareness into your body. Roll your shoulders up and back a couple of times to release tension.

Step 3: Now shuffle back slightly until you're in contact with each other, shifting your legs into a comfortable position. Feel the support of your partner as you soften your breath and close your eyes or lower your gaze.

Step 4: Notice if you can feel the breath of your partner and where it most strongly connects to your own body.

Step 5: After a few rounds of noticing each other's breath, you may begin to sync up to the rhythm of their breath. Notice how this feels to be breathing together.

Step 6: Stay here as long as you both feel comfortable and connected.

Tip: Put on a soothing playlist to aid you in relaxation.

FINAL THOUGHTS

We are all alchemists, with the power to create and transform how we feel when life gets messy. There are universal challenges that we all have to deal with as part of being human, and each of our journeys will look a little different. I invite you to spend time getting familiar with your own wants and needs. Notice how they shift depending on what's going on for you internally, and what's being asked of you externally. Create goals and intentions with wellbeing at the top of your priority list. Design a life that you love.

Make it a regular practice to reflect on the ways you can be more active in caring for yourself and your community beyond the chapters in this book. Be aware of the power of your thoughts, the impact of your words and the consequences of your actions. Honour your body temple by fuelling it with wholesome foods, seasonal fruits and vegetables. Release physical and emotional tension through awareness, mindful movement and intentional breathing. Be conscious of the environments you occupy and the company you keep. Carve out time for activities that light you up and nurture the inner child within. The simplest things can bring us joy and give us a deeper sense of who we are. Put together your own toolkit of rituals that creates lasting fulfilment and inner peace. My biggest plea is that you listen to your body's call to slow down and rest. In hearing your body whisper, you are less likely to cause it to scream.

Life will never be free of challenges and difficulty, and there will be things that arise that even the most radical of self-care won't be able to fix. But in nurturing our inner resilience formed from compassion and worthiness, we can be more empowered and better resourced to face our problems head on. Inevitably there will be times when life requires more of us than we can give. Please always reach out for support when you need it. No one needs to go through this bonkers journey we call life on their own.

Thank you so much for investing your time and energy into reading this book. Transforming ourselves is how we transform the world around us. The revolution begins within! May your radical self-care create radical self-love and a radical aliveness. May you live fully, openly and in full commitment to your purpose. May the ripples of love and nurturance that you create for yourself spread to your families, friends, communities and beyond.

All my love,
Rebecca x

Resources

Recommended Reading

Abbott, Katie. *Love's Secret: A Journey to the Beyond*, Quilliam Press Ltd, Newmarket, 2022.

Ali, Farzana. *Sound Healing*, Watkins Publishing, London, 2024.

Cameron, Julia. *The Artist's Way*, Pan Books, London, 1995.

Dass, Ram. *Be Here Now*, Crown, London, 1971.

Harsono, Jasmin. *Self Reiki*, DK, London, 2019.

Khalsa, Harbhajan Singh. *Kundalini Postures and Poetry*, Tarcherperigree, New York, 2003.

Kindred, Glennie. *Elements of Change*, Central Books, Dagenham, 2009.

LaPorte, Danielle. *The Desire Map*, Sounds True, Colorado, 2014.

Lovatt, Lauren. *Mind Food*, Leaping Hare Press, London, 2022.

Macleod, Isla. *Rituals for Life*, Laurence King, London, 2022.

Nafousi, Roxie. *Manifest*, Michael Joseph, London, 2022.

Nestor, James. *Breath*, Riverhead Books, London, 2020.

Okakura, Kakuzo. *The Book of Tea*, Tuttle, Vermont, 2018.

Osbon, Diane K. (ed.). *A Joseph Campbell Companion: Reflections on the Art of Living*, HarperCollins, New York, 1992.

Pierre, Chloe. *Take Care*, Headline, London, 2023.

Rubin, Rick. *The Creative Act: A Way of Being*, Canongate Books, Edinburgh, 2023.

Ruiz, Don Miguel. *The Four Agreements*, Amber-Allen Publishing, California, 2018.

Somi, Sobonfu. *The Spirit of Intimacy*, William Morrow & Company, New York, 2000.

Tolle, Eckhart. A New Earth, Penguin, London, 2009.

Tolle, Eckart. *The Power of Now*, New World Library, California, 2004.

Moon Tracking Apps

The Moon: apps.apple.com/us/app/the-moon-calendar-moon-phases/

Astro Seek: mooncalendar.astro-seek.com/

Biographies

About the Author

Rebecca Moore is a certified wellness guide, curator and author, with many years of experience teaching groups and individuals how to discover tools for self-healing. As well as breathwork, mindfulness and meditation, Rebecca is also skilled in energy healing, bodywork, and is a member of the global Sacred Fig faculty of yoga teachers. Her work is inspired by alternative medicine and ancient healing modalities adapted to support modern-day city living. Rebecca has a passion for curating empowering projects that inspire connection and love and invite people to feel. She was born and raised in London where she currently resides and holds spaces for herself and others to explore, express and expand.
www.rebecca-moore.com / @_rebecca_moore

About the Illustrator

Amberlee is an illustrator, mental health practitioner and lecturer who lives by the mantra 'you can be more than one thing'. She founded Line & Honey, an illustration studio focused on minimal, intentional design and the visibility of women of colour. Based in London and of Jamaican heritage, she instigates conversations around representation, softness, and how we access rest through her work.
www.lineandhoney.co.uk / @line_and_honey

About the Photographer

Christian Cassiel is a British-Jamaican visual artist who uses photography to navigate the world and build relationships with people and the communities he engages with. The ability to create while understanding the cultural and historical context of his subjects, allows him to produce imagery that is both visually absorbing and emotionally resonant.
www.christiancassiel.com / @christiancassiel

Index

Author Acknowledgements

I am deeply grateful for the magnificent teachers and friends who have inspired the contents of these pages: Eckhart Tolle, Katie Abbott, Bill Cumming, Marina South, Anton Brandt, LiYing Lim, Magdalena Gladstone, Kira Balaskas, Dr Rose Erin Vaughan, Anya Pearse, Vicky Johnson, and my earth angels Shannon Rae Lawes and Sophia Georgiou.

Sending love to my treasured family of cheerleaders: Mum, Dad, Kingsley, Manu, Kyrese, Maria Francesca, and my heartbeat, Rennae.

To my beloved cosmic sister, soul guide and earth angel Cassie Yukawa-McBurney; it was your sacred reminders to practise self-care during some very taxing times that planted the seed for this book. Thank you for your unwavering love, support and encouragement.

To the wonderful and insanely talented Christian Cassiel and Amberlee Green, thank you for blessing this book with your exquisite photography and illustrations. I feel so lucky to have met you both, so organically, whilst exploring birds, nature and community. Big thanks to Flock Together, for bringing us together.

Thank you to Samantha Jones. Drinking cups of Living Tea raised my spirits on the days when writing felt difficult.

A huge thank you to the wonderful team at Leaping Hare and Quarto, with special thanks to the incredible Monica Perdoni.

Thank you to all the teachers and guides, named and unnamed, seen and unseen, known and unknown, who supported the birthing of this book.

We are all wisdom keepers with valuable resources to offer one another. If you have thoughts, ideas or go-to rituals you'd like to share, please get in touch or tag your content with #radicalselfcare #ritualsforinnerresiliance on Instagram.

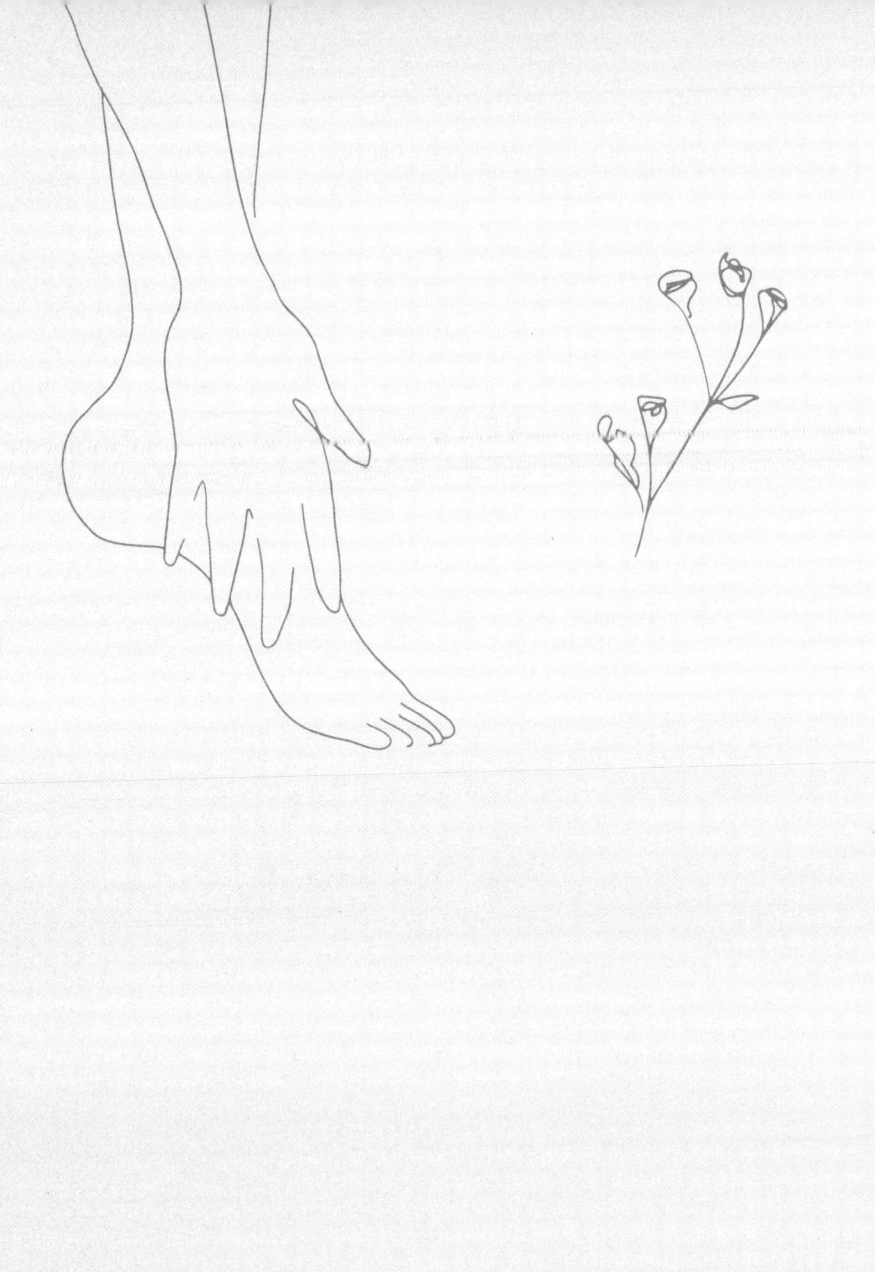